# Born Again to Win

J.Wallace Boyce

WESTBOW
PRESS®
A DIVISION OF THOMAS NELSON
& ZONDERVAN

Unless otherwise noted, scripture quotations are
from the King James Version of the Bible.

WestBow Press books may be ordered through
booksellers or by contacting:

WestBow Press
A Division of Thomas Nelson & Zondervan
1663 Liberty Drive
Bloomington, IN 47403
www.westbowpress.com
1 (866) 928-1240

ISBN: 978-1-5127-0578-2 (sc)
ISBN: 978-1-5127-0579-9 (e)

Library of Congress Control Number: 2015912248

Print information available on the last page.

WestBow Press rev. date: 10/30/2015

# Preface

God created man to live in loving fellowship with Himself for ever as sons of God conformed to the likeness of His only begotten Son the Lord Jesus Christ, who is perfect. Accordingly God created man an eternal being with an intellect, a conscience and a free will so that he could choose to accept the goodness of God.

In the fullness of time God manifested Himself in the person of the Son, the man Christ Jesus that He might provide Himself a Lamb for the burnt offering by which He would give Himself a ransom for all that He might redeem each and every human being from a human nature that is sinful and evil and reconcile all the world unto Himself with a nature that is divine and good.

We who are followers of Christ in times past we walked according to the course of this world. But God who is rich in mercy and for the great love with which He loved us did set aside each of us to bring each to repentance and belief of the gospel. On hearing and believing it pleased God to justify us, and to send the Spirit of His Son into our heart. Each was born again of the Spirit of God into the family of God, and given the new nature of wanting to please God, and also the power to do that which is good and right at all times.

In this book the author sets out to show the right way of doing that which is good and right according to the word of God. It is hoped that it will bring glory and honour to the Lord Our God and be a help and a blessing to the reader.

# Contents

# The Right Mind of Righteousness

Each believer on conversion, having repented and having accepted the person and the work of the Son of God, is by supernatural means born again into the family of God. The moment he believes on the Lord Jesus Christ, God is pleased to adopt him into the family of God, and sends forth the Spirit of His Son into his heart, to plant and establish the desire to live to please God and do right at all times. So the child of God is well equipped to live worthy of his calling and is without excuse in not doing right and not pleasing his heavenly Father. The desire to please his Father, should characterize every child of God. If one lacks that desire, he would be wise to honestly examine himself, whether he be in the faith; prove himself. The sincere desire of the child of God should be to please God and do right at all times, and as it becometh the Son of God to fulfil all righteousness, so also it becometh every adopted son of God to fulfil all righteousness.

It should become him to start by consecrating himself to doing right. This he does in the public place by being baptized in water (totally immersed). In so doing, he is declaring that the sincere desire of his heart is to do right at all times. He is also declaring how he intends to do right; by dying to self and living unto God. He is also obeying our Lord's command to be baptized, and has this assurance from the Lord, that "he that believeth and is baptized shall be saved." This simply means, that he that believes that Jesus Christ is the Son of God, and sincerely wants to do right at all times will be saved from doing wrong and in turn enabled to do right.

In order to do right, one must know what is right in the sight of God; he must grow in the knowledge of the will of God. But in order to know the will of God, one must be willing to do the will of God. He has from the Lord this assurance, "if any man will do His will, he shall know of the doctrine whether it be of God" John 7:17. In order to be willing to do the will of God, he must have a fear of displeasing God. He must have high thoughts of God and poor thoughts of self. He must be of humble mind and poor in spirit to believe the truth. With a mind that is right toward God he will bow to the word of God and will grow in knowing God, and in trusting God, and in turn grow in loving God. Then he will sincerely want to please God, and do what is right at all times.

The child of God that will do the will of God by preaching the gospel to every creature has this assurance from the word of God that, "as many as received Him, to them gave He power to become the sons of God, to them that believe on His name" John 1:12. He can go into the public place and from house to house, teaching and preaching Jesus Christ, speaking forth what he knows to be sound words, the truth, and testifying of what he has seen. He does not believe one thing and say another. He speaks as one having authority, not as the scribes who thought one thing and taught another. His speech is sound and sensible, for sound words are only sounded forth with a sound mind from a sound heart that has soundly seized sound doctrine. Sound doctrine will produce it's own evangel; it cannot be stayed. Like Jeremiah the word of God will be in his heart as a burning fire, he cannot hold it back. It will stir up a simple saint to stand up as a strong servant for the truth of what is right and for our Lord Jesus Christ. He will declare the truth at all times; he will not compromise it to suit his hearers; nor withhold it to avoid hostility. He is not ashamed of the gospel of Christ: for it is the power of God unto salvation to everyone that believeth, and realizing that he is a debtor both to the wise and unwise, he is ready to preach the gospel of the goodness of God with all that is in him to everyone.

Truly "God is good and is good to all." Psalm 145:9. "Great is the Lord, and greatly to be praised; and His greatness is unsearchable." Psalm 145:3. "The Lord is righteous in all His ways, and holy in all His works." Psalm 145:17. God being good and righteous wills to do the greatest good to all and through His people to the greatest number of people, yea to every creature. This is the righteousness of God.

That the good news of the righteousness of God be made known unto the whole world the Lord God commissioned His disciples saying – "go ye therefore, and teach all nations, baptizing them in the name of the Father, and of the Son, and of the Holy Ghost: teaching them to observe all things whatsoever I have commanded you: and, lo, I am with you alway, unto the end of the world." Math.28:19-20. He further told them – "go ye into alll the world, and preach the gospel to every creature. He that believeth and is baptized shall be saved; but he that believeth not shall be damned." The apostle John declared – "But as many as received Him, to them gave He power to become the sons of God, to them that believe on His name: which were born, not of blood, nor of the will of the flesh, nor of the will of man, but of God". John 1:11-13.

A soul that has right thoughts of God will have a right mind of the righteousness of God. He will gladly proclaim "Thou art worthy, O Lord to receive of glory and honour and power for thou hast created all things and for thy pleasure they are and were created."Rev.4:11 He will see God as being perfect, righteousness and wanting to reconcile all unto Himself and working all things together for the good of all that all may be made perfect.

This vision of God wanting to make every one perfect is given by God. The apostle Paul had this vision and toward which he pressed (see Phil.3:12-14,), and "warned every man, and taught every man in all wisdom; that he might present every man perfect in Christ Jesus." Col.1:28. This is the heavenly vision that compelled him to preach the gospel for which he suffered all things and with confidence did gladly say "nevertheless I am not ashamed: for I know whom I have believed and am persuaded that He is able to keep that which I have committed unto Him against that day. Hold fast the form of sound words, which thou hast heard of me, in faith and love which is in Christ Jesus." 2Tim.1:12-13. Having, therefore obtained help of God he continued witnessing both to small and great, saying none other things than those which the prophets and Moses did say should come. This heavenly vision is the right mind of the righteousness of God and leads to right doctrine, that of Adoption, and in turn to right practice.

The Doctrine of Adoption is simply God willing man to come into relationship with Himself, and man willing to come into relationship with God. Whosoever wills to accept the will of God, believes God and it is imputed unto him for righteousness, and God adopts him into the family of God. He is one of that group of people, the elect of God, who willed to accept the will of God. This is the purpose of God according to election. For this purpose God created all. For this purpose "God was in Christ reconciling the world unto Himself, not imputing their transgressions unto them." 2Cor.5:19. Accordingly God would have His people beseech in Christ's stead all to be reconciled unto God and has given us the word of reconciliation.

The doctrine of Adoption gives God the glory of being Sovereign God, who created man in His likeness, an eternal being with an intellect, a conscience and a free will that he might will to choose the will of God. It gives God the honour due to Him, who is righteous, no respecter of persons, just and the justifier of him which believeth in Jesus, and will have mercy and not sacrifice. It gives God the power (right) to judge in righteousness His creation, each and every one that believeth on the Son of God (those that will accept the will of God), and each and every one that believeth not on the Son of God (those that will not accept the will of God). It is from above, pure, then peaceable, gentle, easy to be entreated, full of mercy and good fruits, without partiality, and without hypocrisy. .

The doctrine of Adoption is not only simple it is good; it is of God. For herein God chooses to do good to man by giving him the power (right) to become a child of God, and gives man the right to choose to accept the goodness of God, and become a child of God. The purpose of God according to election is in keeping with the character of God and the doctrine of Adoption is not only good, it is grand, great, and glorious. It is grand, for it is of grandeur purpose than all purposes - as far as the heavens above the earth so is the purpose of adoption above saving man from eternal punishment and even fitting him for a place in heaven. It is great, for it manifests the greatness of God, and is exceedingly abundantly above all that man could think. It is glorious, for it shows forth the glories of God.

The doctrine of Adoption progressively promotes itself from the Position of Adoption in the Purpose of

Adoption by the Process of Adoption to the Prospect of Adoption.

The Position of Adoption - Sonship

Adoption is good, for it expresses the goodness of God in creating man in His own likeness to live in loving fellowship with God for ever as a son of God, conformed to the image of His only begotten Son, who is perfect and did always those things that please God. Adoption to sonship provides privilege, glory, honour, and power to every human being. This inheritance is the birth right of every one, and betokens the love of God to man. It is available to all. Man on choosing to accept the Son of God is given the right to be a child of God. according to John 1:12 – "as many as received Him, to them gave He the power to become the sons of God, to them that believe on His name." He that receives the Lord Jesus Christ in entirety, that is His person and His work, is given the right to become a child of God. Each and every one is capable of believing the truth, so each and every one is capable of becoming a child of God. God holds each and everyone responsible for believing on the Son of God, and receiving the right to become a child of God, and to live worthy of his calling, and to grow in the likeness of our Lord who is perfect. That is the goal. That is the

The Purpose of Adoption - Perfection

Adoption is grand for it's purpose is far above all purposes, namely the perfection of man. The Lord Jesus Christ would have the people of God as the Father, for He exhorted them – "be ye therefore perfect, even as your Father which is in heaven is perfect." Math.5:48. This was the mind and will of God according "as He hath chosen us in Him (Christ) before the foundation of the world, that we should be holy and without blame before Him in love. Having predestinated us unto the adoption of children by Jesus Christ to himself, according to the good pleasure of his will" Ephes.1:4-5.

Before the foundation of the world God planned to create man to please Himself and purposed to adopt all that would believe in His Son and to conform them to the image of the Son of God, the perfect one, to the praise of the glory of His grace, wherein He hath made us accepted in the beloved. By virtue of His grace, God perfects in His sight those that are sanctified through the offering of the body of Jesus Christ. This is positional sanctification.

By that same grace God will perfect His own and having sanctified one to become a child of God and be perfect, God will progressively sanctify him by the Spirit of God, through the word of God, and empower him to walk as becomes a child of God, living to please God doing right at all times and going on to perfection, that is

The Process of Adoption – Progressive Sanctification

'We are bound to give thanks alway to God for you, brethren beloved of the Lord, because God hath from the beginning chosen you to salvation through sanctification of the Spirit and belief of the truth Whereunto He called you by our gospel, to the obtaining of the glory of our Lord Jesus Christ." 2Thes.2:13-14. This is the process of progressive sanctification that God choose for the heirs of salvation, by which God would save man from further sinning against God and doing further evil. Sanctification is of the Lord. It is the Lord God making known truth unto man and man accepting it: that is the just living by faith. It is the Lord God saving each child of God to the uttermost.

When God perfects a soul in His sight, and adopts him into the family of God, that is his standing, and God the Father requires him to make perfection his goal. God gives him the power to apprehend that for which he has been apprehended. Even though he has this perfect standing with God, his manner of living is not perfect, so he must follow after perfection; he must count not himself to have apprehended, but forgetting those things which are behind and reaching forth unto things which are before, one thing he must press toward the mark for the prize of the high calling of God in Christ Jesus. God will set him apart to perfect him, to shape him into doing right by showing him what is right and enabling him to do right. On hearing and hearkening to the word of God he will be exercised toward righteousness and be saved continuously from doing wrong. He will be being changed. With the image of the Lord ever before him, and wanting to be like Him, he with open face beholding as in a glass the glory of the Lord, will be changed into the same image from glory to glory, as by the Spirit of the Lord. "Now we who are sons of God, it doth not yet appear what we shall be: but we know that, when He shall appear, we shall be like Him; for we shall see Him as He is."1John3:2 Then, we shall apprehend that for which we have been apprehended - perfection, the glory of our Lord Jesus Christ, in the perfect environment of heaven, fulfilling our purpose of being created enjoying perfect fellowship with our Lord Jesus Christ and His creation that is

The Prospect of Adoption – Perfected Sanctification

Oh, the riches of His glory on the vessels of mercy, which He had afore prepared unto glory, even us whom He hath called, not of the Jews only, but of the gentiles. "For whom He did foreknow, He also did predestinate conformed to the image of His Son, that He might be the first born among many brethren. Moreover whom He did predestinate, them He also called: and whom He called, them He also justified: and whom He justified, them He also glorified." Rom.8:30. Poor, depraved creatures, not worthy of the least favor, yet God has shown mercy on us that repented and believed on His Son. Yes, we who willed to accept the will of God.

What shall we say then ? Unrighteousness with God ? God forbid. Rightly did God say to Moses – "I will have mercy on whom I will have mercy, and I will have compassion on whom I will have compassion." Rom.9:15, and the Lord God said – "I will have mercy and not sacrifice. "Math.9:13. God will have mercy and not sacrifice His character of being righteous and no respecter of persons and His judgment will be righteous.

It is right to punish a wrongdoer that will not repent: but it also right to show mercy and pardon a wrongdoer (malefactor) that will repent. God is righteous and doeth right. God knows those that will not obey the word of the Lord (will not to do the will of God) and repent and believe on the Son of God. He will judge them rightly and will punish them with everlasting destruction from the presence of the Lord and the glory of His power. God who created all things, is Sovereign ruler over His creation. He has the Sovereign right to make one vessel unto honour and another unto dishonor; just as the potter hath power over the clay. God knows those who will repent and believe the word of God and He will show them mercy and pardon and raise them up as vessels unto honor and glory. What a glorious prospect for each child of God (those that will to accept the will of God) – "in the twinkling of an eye, at the last trump: for the trumpet shall sound, and the dead shall be raised incorruptible, and we shall be changed 1Cor.15:52. For the Lord himself shall descend from heaven with a shout, with the voice of the archangel, and with the trump of God: and the dead in Christ shall rise first:

then we which are alive and remain shall be caught up together with them in the clouds, to meet the Lord in the air: and so shall we ever be with the Lord." 1Thes.4:16-17. Wherefore we comfort one another with these words and with the prospect of beholding and sharing His glory, the perfections of the Perfect One in the perfect environment of heaven, fulfilling our purpose of being created, and enjoying living in perfect fellowship with God and His creation. That will be paradise.

With such a glorious prospect in view, and knowing that we were chosen to be perfect in love, we would make perfect love our goal and be as He in this world, and with the same mind that was in our Lord Jesus Christ and with the heavenly vision of God doing the greatest good to the greatest number of people by reconciling the world unto Himself and perfecting every one, we would humbly go forth to pass the time of our sojourning in the fear of our Lord and cease not to beseech each and every one to be reconciled unto God and live to fulfill the purpose of being created.

# The Right Means of Righteousness

Our Lord Jesus Christ knows, that of ourselves we could not fulfil the purpose for which we have been created, and that we need the gracious help of the Holy Spirit. He did comfort His followers saying – "let not your heart be troubled: ye believe in God, believe also in me. In my Father's house are many mansions: if not, I would have told you. I go to prepare a place for you that where I am ye may be also" and did comfort them further intimating – "I will pray the Father, and He shall give you another Comforter, that He may abide with you for ever" John 14:1-2, 16. Now, the Comforter, the Holy Spirit came from above to abide with the people of God to do them good and with their cooperation do good to others. Having righteousness imputed to them, God through the Holy Spirit inputs righteousness into each child of God. He imparts to each and every one born again into the family of God the divine nature, with a love for God and His creation, and with the desire to do right and please God. In order to fulfil that desire, the Holy Spirit will not only show him the truth of what is right, but will strive with him to accept it and empower him to do it, that He might guide him into fulfilling all righteousness.

There shall be opposition; the enemy will not allow righteousness to have it's free course, but will seek to stop it. So, it is of paramount importance that the servant of God knows his enemy and is not ignorant of his devices. The child of God needs not only the Holy Spirit to be with him at all times, but to be in complete control of him, for He will uphold him in the battle and make him to triumph just as He did when our Lord was tempted by the devil to act independent of the Father. For the child of God to go forth in his own strength it is utter folly; he is bound to fail.

The work is the Lord's. It is the Lord, that is doing good, and He does it by His Spirit indwelling and ministering righteousness in and through the child of God. The battle is the Lord's, and so is the victory, the honour and the glory. However, the servant of God is subject to like passions as Elijah. He can fail and instead of relying on the Lord he can slip into dwelling on what could happen on the morrow. The fear of the unknown can press in on him and press him down into depression and there he can imagine that he has had enough; he can't take any more and may even want to end it all. The Holy Spirit will lay aside such a devilish desire, and lay him down to sleep under his depression and when he is well rested, He will awaken and comfort him with food and drink, for the journey is too great for him to go it alone. Having comforted him in the Lord, by feeding him on the greatness and goodness of the Lord, and having given him to drink of the love of our Lord for him, the Holy Spirit will encourage him to go forth. He will go forth strengthened in the inner parts, meat for the journey, and with his ear ever open to the still small voice of the Holy Spirit, who will lead him aright and protect him from all evil. But in order to guide the child of God safely, the Holy Spirit must be in control of him or her.

The Lord Jesus Christ, after He was taken up, through the Holy Ghost gave commandments unto the apostles whom He had chosen and through the apostle Paul commanded His people as recorded in the epistle to the Ephesians to walk worthy of their vocation (4:1); in love (5:2); as children of light (5:8), and circumspectly (5:15), not as fools, but as wise, redeeming the time because the days are evil. "Wherefore be ye not unwise, but understanding what the will of the Lord. And be not drunk with wine, wherein is excess; but be filled with the Spirit" Eph, 5:15-18. This command 'to be filled' is not a once for all time operation. It means to be being filled, and is an on going operation whereby the child of God is being filled continuously. He is being continuously controlled and empowered by the Holy Spirit, who will renew his mind with the knowledge of the will of God, and control and empower him to do the will of God. The Spirit of God will enable the people of God to submit themselves one to another in the fear of God.

It might sadden some selfish sister to submit to her husband as unto the Lord, the Spirit of God will enable her to do so joyfully, and furthermore add to her faith virtue, knowledge, self-control, holiness, kindness and love. These things will abound in her and she shall be neither barren nor unfruitful in the knowledge of our Lord Jesus Christ. She shall be sober and faithful in all things. She'll stand up for what she knows is right and that which brings honor to her God and her family, for she shall bring up her children in the nurture of the Lord. She'll not have an idle moment, for all her time will be profitably spent in caring for her household. She'll be wise in her speech, for she'll know when to speak and when not, and she'll rightly speak of what she knows and will do so with grace and kindness. She will be of great value, yea more than rubies. She'll be precious to her husband, and he shall safely trust her. She'll do him good and no evil all the days of her life. She'll be known and respected in the neighbourhood

The sister that hath an unbelieving husband, will seek to be in subjection to him so that he may without the word be won. She'll be known not by the outward adorning of the hair or her fashionable apparel, but by a meek and quiet spirit, which in the sight of God is of great price, and comes from the indwelling Spirit being in control.

Then again, there is the sister, that hath an unbelieving husband, and she seeks to be in subjection to him and do well, but is afraid with terror. She is known as a martyr and respected for her faith. She is married to a worthless fellow. He leaves her at home to go down to the tavern to sit down to eat and drink, then rise up to play with other men's wives, adorned with plaited hair, wearing gold and dressed like Jezebel. He returns home to shamefully treat his wife, and wickedly kick and beat her. Her suffering is known only to her and her God, who would have her be in subjection to her husband, that he may without the word be won by her conversation. She will weep bitterly and cry out unto the Lord until she has no more power to cry. Such an one needs divine help. When her suffering becomes more than she can bear, and she is minded to leave and take her children with her, she will question within herself -*'is it lawful to leave?'*. Then she will look to the word of God for guidance and read – "and the woman who hath an husband that believeth not, and if he be pleased to dwell with her, let her not leave him" 1Cor7:13. She needs to be filled with the Spirit to discern if it please her husband to dwell with her.

The brethren that have unbelieving wives are to dwell with them according to knowledge, as unto the weaker vessel, and as being heirs together of the grace of life 1Pet.3:7. They are to have compassion, love as brethren, pitiful, courteous, not rendering evil for evil, or railing, but on the contrary render blessing, knowing that we are called to this, that we should inherit a blessing. Such grace comes from the gracious help of the Holy Spirit controlling that brother.

Then, there is the brother that seeks to be righteous, and do right, but is vexed sorely every day by his wife lusting after other men. She does not render unto him benevolence and will defraud him. Harlotry, wine and new wine hath taken away her heart, and he who she once desired she now detests and would destroy. When she goes forth in the evening to meet her lovers that dine her, dress her and drink with her, he remains at home with his thoughts. He is no fool that suspects the worst, yet God would have him think no evil. He can't do so, in his own strength: he needs the help of the Spirit of God to control him, and keep him from thinking evil, and enable him to think good by fixing his mind on things above and solely on the Lord, who will keep him in perfect peace.

When she returns in the early hours of the morning, he can greet her with words seasoned with grace, rather than spiked with the poison of asps. In the fulness of guilt and hatred she may poison her children against him, and together they may treat that brother cruelly, shamefully and viciously, even desiring his end. He will soon learn by experience the truth, *that a man's foes shall be they of his own household.* It is remarkable that she who is the worst wife, may be the perfect mate; the perfect one for God to use, in perfecting that which is lacking in him. Yes, the Lord who loveth that brother will chasten him by exercising him to do that which grieves him to do - love his wife. Nevertheless, afterward it will yield the peaceable fruit of righteousness unto him.

One such brother spent much time in the private place pouring out his soul, with many tears, yet his words were few - *please help.* God is faithful, He will not suffer one to be tempted above that he is able: but will with the temptation also make a way to escape, that he may be able to bear. Within days, God permitted the devil to incite that brother's family to put him out of the house. The pain of having to leave all for which he had given his all, was unspeakable. It was then the Comforter drew nigh to uphold him and enable him to accept in all humility that which he couldn't change, and very quietly he took his belongings and took his leave to go where he knew not, but knew He that lead him, would lead him aright. As he left that place, the Holy Spirit went ahead to another brother, to open his heart and his house to that rejected brother, and whilst he went forth, he was minded to go to his friend, who on hearing, welcomed and comforted him with the comfort with which he had been comforted. Truly, he being in the way the Spirit lead him. God will not permit His people to suffer unduly, but only that which He can use for their good. In the years that followed, God has worked all things together for good to that brother, and he is quick to confess that it was good for him to have to leave his own, and to them he is able to say - *ye meant it for evil, but God meant it for good.*

The Holy Spirit enabled him that had been put away by his wife to live as though he had no wife, and not to seek another, and when taken unaware by a strange woman with strange ideas, seeking to have him, he did not behave himself improperly, but was in control of himself, knowing how to possess his vessel in sanctification and honour. Even when one took hold of him, the Holy Spirit maintained a greater hold on him and enabled him to withstand in the evil day and remain standing. Such trials and temptations and tribulations and persecutions make it grievous for that brother to love his wife; yet he is commanded to love her as Christ loved the Church and gave Himself for it. The Holy Spirit will enable him to forgive her and obey that commandment.

Such trials and temptations and tribulations and persecutions may never be experienced by brethern that have married in the Lord, yet it might grieve some brethern to love their wives even as Christ loved the Church and gave Himself for it. The Spirit of God will enable that brother to overcome his grief, if he grieve not the Holy Spirit, and will enable him to control himself, and his house, and to be sober and sensible, of good behaviour, given to hospitability, apt to teach; not given to wine, no striker, not given to filthy lucre, but patient, not a brawler, not covetous; one that ruleth well his own house having his children in subjection with all gravity.

It is right for children to obey their parents in the Lord. Yes, it is wise to '*honor thy father and mother*' for it is the first commandment with a promise. But there are children who are rebels without a cause. They are without wisdom. They are without a promise. But they are not without help.

It is natural for the unmarried to want to marry, but every one has his gift, one after this manner of remaining unmarried and another after that manner of marrying. Paul was permitted to make this judgment that it is good for them to abide as he, unmarried, untroubled in the flesh, uncaring for the things of this world, and unhindered in caring for the things that belong to the Lord. If they cannot control themselves then let them marry, for it is better to marry than burn. They that try to control themselves will fail. They need to be filled with the Spirit, then they can exercise self control. In so doing they will avoid weeping and gnashing of the teeth. Oh, the shame and sorrow when a young sister makes known to the oversight her lack of foresight and self-control in yielding to temptation.

Likewise, the young brother or sister may marry one outside the family of God, and live to regret it every day of his or her life. It is wise for the child of God seeking a partner to be filled with the Spirit and lead aright to the partner of God's choosing. It is unwise to imagine that there is nothing worse than not getting a partner. There is! Getting the wrong partner. So, be wise and be filled with the Spirit.

There are many of God's people going home in hope-mobiles, hoping they will be protected from all trials, and temptations and tribulations and harm along the way, and from a distance be able to see all that takes place, without experiencing it themselves. They have never sat where others are sitting, and cannot sorrow with those that sorrow. They know nothing of the comfort of God in tribulation and are not able to comfort them which are in any trouble, by the comfort wherewith they have been comforted of God. They are hoping to make it through this vale of tears without shedding any and without suffering persecution. They think that the text of Heb.2:3 - *how shall we escape if we neglect so great salvation*, is a warning to the unsaved and applies to salvation from eternal woe. But there are some of God's people who know that it is a great salvation, that is fully comprehensive, and goes beyond salvation from eternal punishment, and that it takes in salvation from the power of sin, and also from the power of satan. Such are sober and vigilant and wise to take earnest heed to things which they have heard, lest at any time they should let slip and not only transgress the will of God, but also let slip any of God's promises of help and protection, and slip out of the rest of God and slip away from the Lord and slip into the way of the devil their adversary, who as a roaring lion, walketh about, seeking whom he may devour.

Moment by moment they rely solely upon the Lord to be with them in their troubles and to uphold them, and deliver them and show them His salvation. The servant, that God has chosen to refine in the furnace of affliction will not confine his preaching of salvation to deliverance from judgment, but will make sure to include deliverance from the power of sin, and from the power of Satan and from all evil that man would do him.

The Lord knows all. He knows whom He can raise up and refine for certain purposes. He foreknew Jeremiah for our Lord told him saying – "before I formed thee in the belly I knew thee; and before thou camest forth out of the womb I sanctified thee, I ordained thee a prophet unto the nations."Jer.1:5. The apostle Paul knew that it pleased God, who separated him from his mother's womb and called by His grace, to reveal His Son in him, that he might preach Him among the heathen. Immediately he conferred not with flesh and blood: neither went he up to Jerusalem to them that were apostles, but he went into Arabia and returned again unto Damascus. The Lord does not make mistakes, and when the risen Lord gives an evangelist to the church, He knows that He wont be disappointed. He knows that He can use that servant as He wills. For He knows that he will fearlessly bear witness to the truth at all times, not compromising it to suit his hearers or withholding it to avoid hostility, and He can send him to the uttermost part of the world, yea even where he may encounter the uttermost hostility. He will not fail. He will have the Spirit of God give to him that He has chosen, the gift of telling forth, and a genuine concern for the welfare of others, and a genuine desire to do the work.

There are those who desire to be evangelists, yet the Lord has given them as teachers, and the Holy Spirit has given them the gift of teaching, they have gladly and gratefully accepted their privilege. Time has proven God to be right and that brother is quick to acknowledge the wisdom and goodness of God. Likewise there are those who have wanted to be teachers, and the Lord has given them as evangelists to the Church, and the Holy Spirit has given them the gift of telling forth the goodness of God who has used them for the purpose of evangelising that part of the world, and they have lived to give God the glory.

Many of God's people desire to be evangelists and will go to the uttermost part of the world to preach but they wont go from house to house or from hut to hut teaching and preaching Jesus Christ. They don't desire the work of an evangelist, nor will they suffer the shame, scorn and reproach of sinners. Likewise there are those who desire to be shepherds and teachers, but they don't want the work. They want the position, the power, the prominence, but not the persecution, that such Godly men shall suffer.

The Lord knows all and knows what is in man, and He knows the child of God that He can use and how He can use him, and so those He has chosen to use as evangelists He will call. All of God's people are called by the gospel to do right and please God, but it pleases God to choose a few for special purposes. Those few chosen will have the character and blend of attributes for the particular purpose. This is known only to God and the Lord will ordain each for the purpose chosen. Now the Spirit of God would not have us ignorant concerning spiritual gifts. "There are diversities of gifts, but the same Spirit. and there are differences of administrations, but the same Lord. and there are diversities of operations, but it is the same God which worketh all in all. For to one is given by the Spirit the word of wisdom; to another the word of knowledge by the same Spirit; to another faith by the same Spirit; to another the gifts of healing by the same Spirit; to another the working of miracles; to another prophecy; to another discerning of spirits; to another [divers] kinds of tongues; to another the interpretation of tongues: But all these worketh that one and the selfsame Spirit, dividing to every man severally as he will." 1Cor.12:4-11. So that each child of God has received a gift, and will be held responsible for using it. It behoves each to discern that gift, and exercise it. Therefore he must needs be filled with the Spirit.

It is wise for brethren seeking to worship God to be filled with the Spirit, so that He may move each of them to sacrifice much time to get alone with God. There He will take of the things of the Lord and occupy their minds with the greatness, goodness and love of the Lord. When they come together in one place on the first day of the week, it is to remember the Lord. The Spirit of the Lord will take control of the meeting, and having control of the brethern will take each brother as He will, to bring forth his exercise concerning the things of the Lord, so that they all (brothers and sisters) may feed on the greatness and goodness of the Lord, and drink in of His love, and be edified. With such sacrifice of praise, God is well pleased. With such sacrifice of praise the devil is not pleased. He does not want the saints to worship God, and will try to hinder and stop us doing so. As we are enjoining and enjoying the exercises of the brethren in whom the word of God dwells richly, and who appear to be gifted in ordering and expressing their thoughts so admirably, he will fill our heads with foolish imagining that we have not been so gifted. So, we will leave it to these brethren to speak forth praises.

This is no reason for not offering praise unto God. It is an excuse!

Every brother is well able to offer the sacrifice of praise. But in order to do so, he must purpose to sacrifice time to prepare an offering. When we purpose to do so, the devil will keep us so busy that we won't have time to get alone with God, and so we will have nothing to offer at the memorial feast. Even when we have prepared, and the Holy Spirit exercises us to bring forth our offering, he will tempt us to pass up the opportunity by filling our heads with doubt that we are not fully prepared, and with fear of making a fool of ourselves by saying something improper. To yield to the devil's tempting is sin and grieves the Spirit.

Then again, the flesh may press one to say something, taking no thought how or what he shall say, but taking for granted that the Holy Spirit shall teach him in the self same hour, what he ought to say. Such is the offering of a fool, for it is not only folly but it is sin to put the Spirit of God to the test. However, the Holy Spirit is gracious and will provide a way for that one to excuse himself. Let us be wise and not tempt the Lord our God, lest He confound us before our brethren.

If we have nothing to say, then we should say nothing. But in order to have something to say, something to offer then we should take time to get alone with God, and seek an exercise of love to offer. God will not disappoint. The Holy Spirit will occupy our minds with the greatness and goodness of our Lord, and may require us to sacrifice much time during the week or weeks to perfect our offering. It costs to worship, and we must be like David who said to Araunah nay, - "but I will surely buy of thee at a price; neither will I offer burnt offerings unto the Lord my God of that which doth cost me nothing."2Sam.24:24.

We must not be like Saul who was intent on offering of the sheep and of the oxen that were taken from others, even though they were the best cf.1Sam.15:15., and use another brother's offering that we deem better than our own. Nor should we pick up our offering at the house of God, by picking on a few verses from a hymn, for such worship is not true but is for the purpose of selling ones self, and is making the House of God a place of merchandise. God's earthly people did that and the Lord cast them out, so also will He cast out such worship.

God's earthly people could not offer the same oxen or sheep; for once offered it was consumed. Neither should God's heavenly people dare to make the same offering twice. Yet there are those who repeat it so often that another could make the same offering for them in their absence. It behoves us to offer nothing but the best. God required this of His earthly people (Exod.12:5,6.), and requires no less of His heavenly people. We are without excuse!

The Lord our God is worthy to be praised and loved, and to receive glory, honour, and power, for He hath created us and redeemed us to God by His own blood. We must not rob God of true worship, and we ought not to let the devil rob us of this great privilege. In order to worship God in spirit and in truth we must be filled with the Holy Spirit. Then we can offer the sacrifice of praise to God continually, that is the fruit of the lips giving thanks to His name. This is a sacrifice with which God is well pleased.

To do good and communicate, we must not forget is another sacrifice with which God is well pleased. Sisters should seek to daily bear witness unto our Lord in their neighbourhood, and in order to speak a word in season they must needs be controlled and empowered by the Spirit. Those with children will be kept busy nurturing them in the Lord and have less time to prophesy, whilst those without children will be like Philip's daughters and speak forth as allowed of the Lord to every one that meets them.

The brethren likewise should daily seek to bear witness unto our Lord as they travel to and from their place of employment, and wherever they meet souls. In their neighbourhood they should seek to do the work of an evangelist by going from house to house teaching and preaching Christ Jesus. Each brother needs to be empowered by the Holy Spirit to endure the contradiction of sinners, and to suffer for His name. He needs to be controlled by the Spirit to be as gentle as a dove with all lowliness and meekness to deal with souls, and he needs to be as wise as a serpent to protect his testimony. As he goes forth the Holy Spirit will make him to realize the wisdom of our Lord in sending His disciples two by two, and the absolute necessity of being controlled and empowered by the Spirit of God.

The work of an evangelist is dangerous and demanding, but that does not excuse the servant of God from going forth on his own. If he cannot find a suitable partner, He must go. Woe unto him if he preach not the gospel. Woe unto us, if we preach not the gospel. So, let us make ourselves all things to all that by all means some may be saved through us. Let us be servants unto all, yet not the servants of any, for we are bought with a price. Let us be bond servants of the Lord Jesus Christ, and know what the will of the Lord, and be filled with the Spirit of the Lord.

It is wise for the brethren to be filled with the Spirit of God so that the Holy Spirit may exercise a brother to bring a word from God to the people of God in the presence of the Lord. That spirit filled brother will discern between the leading of the Spirit and the prompting of the flesh, and will minister in the Spirit, a word of doctrine, reproof, correction or instruction in love for the Lord and the Lord's sake, in love for the brethren and to the profit of the people of God and the glory of God.

However, no assembly is perfect, and it has been known for brethren to minister in the flesh. At the remembrance feast of our Lord the worship may have risen to a great height; the brethren raised into the heavenlies, only to be plunged down into a sea of 'I's. There they suffer to the end and separate, some saddened, some sorrowful, and some sickened. When a brother repeatedly refers to himself, does not the scriptures say – "he that speaketh of himself seeketh his own glory." John 7:18. But the scriptures also warn *"that no flesh should glory in His presence." 1Cor.1:29*

Ministry in the flesh is not of God. It dishonours God; it denies Lordship to the Son of God; it denies sovereigny to the Spirit of God; it denies profit to the people of God. It is dangerous for it can be divisive. It is devoid of reward. It is unwise. It is not the will of the Lord. "Wherefore, be ye not unwise but understanding what the will of the Lord, and be not drunk with wine wherein is excess, but be filled with the Spirit." Ephes.5:17,18. This is a command from the risen Lord, and should not be grievous. It should be the desire of each and every child of God, to be filled with the Spirit, controlled and empowered by the Spirit, that he may know and do the will of God.

Now the indwelling Spirit will not take control of a child of God against his will. That child of God must first of all desire to do the will of God, then desire to be filled with the Spirit. He or she must make their desire known unto God, and in order to do so, must draw nigh unto God. Before he does so, he must seek cleansing from all defilement. He can do so with the assurance that - "If we confess our sins He is faithful and just to forgive us our sins and to cleanse us from all unrighteoussness."1John 1:9. The Holy Spirit will not take control of an unclean vessel, nor one that is marred and tarnished with hypocrisy or heresy. Nor will He take control of one that is full of self or partially full of self. It must be empty. There must be an emptying of self, of self will, of the desires of the flesh and of the mind. There must be a sacrificing of the desire of the ears to hear, of the eyes to see, of the tongue to taste, of the mouth to say, of the feet to go, and the mind to think, that which is not pleasing to God. There must be a surrender of one's time, talents, and treasure.

**There is a price to be paid for being filled with the Spirit. There is a greater price to be paid for not being filled with the Spirit.** see ch.10.

In order to count the cost the child of God must sacrifice much time each day searching his soul in order to get to the heart of the matter, which is the heart, and know for sure that it is the desire of his heart to do the will of God whatever the cost. This requires wisdom. If any one lacks wisdom, "let him ask of God, that giveth to all men liberally and upbraideth not; and it shall be given unto him. But let him ask in faith, nothing wavering. For he that wavereth is like a wave of the sea driven with the wind and tossed. For let not that man think that he shall receive any thing of the Lord. A double minded man is unstable in all his ways." James 1:5-8. When the child of God is firmly persuaded in his own mind that he will do the will of God whatever the cost, then he can present his body a living sacrifice, holy, acceptable unto God, which is his reasonable service. God will accept his offering. The Spirit of God will take control of him, and transform him by the renewing of his mind, so that he may not only know that good and perfect will of God, but will do it and prove it. c/f Rom.12:1,2.

The Spirit-filled child of God will go forth from the place of the Holy, delighting in the Lord and knowing for sure that he is filled with the Spirit. He will walk in the Spirit worthy of his vocation, in love, as a child of light, circumspectly, and will walk in a manner that is well pleasing to the Lord, manifesting love, joy, peace, longsuffering, gentleness, goodness, faith, meekness, temperance, and seek to do right at all times.

# The Right Motive of Righteousness

The Spirit filled child of God being lead by the Spirit of God will behave himself as a son of God, "for as many as are led by the Spirit of God, they are the sons of God and The Spirit himself beareth witness with our spirit, that we are the children of God." Rom.8:14-16. We have not received the spirit of bondage again to fear, but we have received the Spirit of adoption, whereby we cry Abba, Father, and God hath given us the Spirit of power, and of love, and of a sound mind, whereby we can behave as sons of God, loving God with all our hearts, mind and soul, and loving our neighbours as ourselves. God the holy Spirit will put righteousness into each and every one to whom God has imputed righteousness. He will impart to him the divine nature, with the desire to please God and do right. The indwelling Spirit will constrain each son of God to love God and to love his neighbour and do right to him. He will love to do that which pleases the Father, and fear doing anything that displeases God. "Knowing therefore the fear (Newberry margin) of the Lord we persuade men." (2Cor.5:11). It is not the fear of judgment, but the fear of displeasing God that motivates the sons of God to go forth to persuade others, and it emanates from our love of God.

This love, that is begotten in the heart of each and every son of God is from God; it is from above and above all love that is begotten in this world. God is its source, nothing can stop its course, nor stay its force. We, who are born of the Spirit of God into the family of God, know that the Son of God loved us and gave Himself for us, and we should love Him because He first loved us. However the child of God, of himself cannot love God or his neighbour. He must realize, that without the Lord enabling he can do nothing. Even though we seek to do right in ministering the word of reconciliation to our neighbours, we cannot influence one, if we lack love. We don't need to declare - '*friend, with all the love that is within this heart of mine, I plead with you in Christ's stead, be ye reconciled unto God*'. We need the gracious help of the Holy Spirit not only to love God and our neighbours, but to move each to consider our counsel. The soul in need can perceive if we say it in love or not. Each of us should come to realize "Though I speak with the tongues of men and of angels, and have not love, I am become sounding brass, or a tinkling cymbal. And though I have prophecy and understand all mysteries, and all knowledge and though I have all faith, so that I could remove mountains, and have not love, I am nothing. And though I bestow all my goods to feed, and though I give my body to be burned, and have not love, it profiteth me nothing." 1Cor.13:1-3.

Most preachers can speak with much gusto, power, zeal, and much noise, and they impress most, even the people of God will rejoice saying - *'that was powerful preaching'*. But, if he does not say it in love, then he is like sounding brass that deafens one's ears so that he cannot distinguish the good from the bad. If on the other hand, fearing to upset those that hear, one says it softly, yet without love he will not stir up anyone; he'll be like a tinkling cymbal making sweet music to the ear that tickles and tingles, but does not trouble them. The child of God may have received from God the gifts of great knowledge and understanding of the scriptures, and may have the gift of prophecy (speaking forth), and have great faith, yet without love he is nothing. They are ineffectual if not exercised in love. Furthermore, the child of God may sacrifice all his possessions, and even himself in doing good to others, yet it is all in vain if it is not done in love. "To obey is better than sacrifice." 1Sam.15:22 It is better to obey our Lord' command – "be filled with the Spirit" Eph. 5:18 then one can obey God's command to love God with all his heart, mind, and soul, and love his neighbour as himself and speak the truth in love.

The Holy Spirit will control the servant of God, so that he will not behave himself unseemly as a son of thunder, nor timidly as a white livered weakling, but in love will declare fearlessly, fervently. firmly, forthrightly facts from the word of God which the Holy Spirit will use to confront sinners, to open the ears of their understanding and trouble them as to their way of living. John the Baptist was such a servant; he was great in the sight of God, though he did no miracle, for he was filled with the Spirit from birth and all that he said of our Lord was true. He feared not man that could kill the body yet not the soul, but feared rather God who can destroy both body and soul in hell, and he fearlessly declared the truth at all times. He stood up for that which is right, and suffered for the cause of righteousness even unto death, reproving all including the King of that which is unlawful. Yet he did it in love. John loved to render honour to whom honour was due saying – "there cometh one mightier than I after me, the latchet of whose shoes I am not worthy to stoop down and unloose," John 1:27 and he pointed them to the Lamb of God.

Truly our Lord was mightier than John, for in Him dwelleth the fulness of the Godhead bodily. He being given the Spirit not by measure, did right at all times by the right means and for the right motive - love. Truly He did say "that the world may know that I love the Father, and, as the Father gave me commandment, even so I do." John 14:51 When He came into this world the Lord said – "Lo, I come, in the volume of the book it is written of me to do thy will O God." Heb.10:7. Great was His purpose in coming into this world; to do the will of God the Father, in manifesting God in the flesh and in providing for man's redemption, reconciliation, salvation and eternal blessing. The Lord loved righteousness, and consecrated Himself to fulfilling all righteousness, and the Father declared His pleasure. Our Lord went forth to declare righteousness, and hid not righteousness within His heart; He sought to manifest the righteousness of God in His dealings with and through man.

God the father gave Him twelve companions, to do good to them and hopefully through them, in spite of their shortcomings, and weaknesses. He suffered them long, for He loved them unto the end. We who are coworkers with our Lord should suffer our brethren in spite of their shortcomings and weaknesses, and love them unto the end, and go forth to love our neighbour and suffer reproach for His name, so that some may be saved.

Our Lord in love for all souls thirsted to do favours to all without respect of persons, and without ceasing. He went out off His way to be kind to one who thirsted for love, life, and happiness. He thirsted to do her a favour, she did not deserve, nor could deserve. We know, that none deserve the slightest favour from God, and that includes us. But for the grace of God we'd still be without hope and without God in this world. Only God knows how far down we would have got into the depths of depravity or if we would be down in the torments of hades. Not only are we debtors to mercy, but we are also debtors to both the wise and the unwise, and so we should show mercy to all, and cease not to be kind and do favours to all. They that are kind to others will not envy them.

Our Lord did not envy others. He did not envy John the Baptist, but gave honor to whom honor was due, for

He said "amongst them that are born of women there hath not risen a greater than John theBaptist."Math.11:11. Every child of God has received gift from God, for there are diversities of gifts and the Holy Spirit divides to every man severally as he will. The child of God, that loves the brethren will not envy another brother or his gift, but will render that due and will encourage him to stir up the gift within him. Unfortunately, many of God's people envy other brethren, especially those engaged in public ministry. The door to door evangelists are not troubled so. Nobody envies their gift. No body wants it, for there is no glory in their work. We servants of God will not waste time envying the Lord's gifts to the Church, but appreciate and use them, and be ever using God given time more profitably, engaging others in conversation regarding faith in Christ. We will not let the possessions of others possess us, and especially those of whom we are seeking to win. Our minds will be solely occupied in wooing and winning our neighbour. We must not be preoccupied with self and think more highly of ourselves than he ought, for that can lead to boasting.

Our Lord did not boast of being mightier than John the Baptist, nor did He tell those to whom He had done good, to go and tell others, nor did He hope they would, but gave them strict instructions to tell no man. We servants of God know that in us is no good thing, and that we are no better than those to whom we speak. We will follow the Lord in not boasting of ourselves, and in not broadcasting our exploits. The Holy Spirit will restrain us from glorying in ourselves and enable us to tell others of the goodness of God, and to glory in the cross of our Lord Jesus Christ. He that seeks not his own glory, will not be puffed up with pride.

Our Lord was not puffed up with pride. He did not pride Himself in being above others, yet He was. He that came from above, is above all. He was above all in thought, word and deed. He was above saying anything that would offend or doing anything that would hurt. Likewise we servants of the Lord will not be puffed up with self and will not be given to behaving unseemly by raising our voice to win arguments. We will seek to control ourselves and behave properly.

Our Lord did not behave Himself unseemly "He did not cry out or cause His voice to be heard in the street." Isa 42:2 He was gentle and meek and behaved properly as becometh the Son of God. We servants of God will walk worthy of our vocation; with all lowliness and meekness with longsuffering we will be courteous and considerate to others. We will attend to what they have to say and discern their needs. Only then can we care for them and their welfare and seek to pour in the oil of comfort.

Our Lord did not seek His own, but always the welfare of others, even in time of danger when those that hated Him without a cause stopped and stooped to gather up stones to cast at Him, He stopped and stooped to spit on the ground and make clay of the spittle and anoint the eyes of one blind from birth and then charge him to go wash in the pool of Siloam. That poor man felt the Master's touch, sensed His concern and care, and his heart was touched and he trusted the Lord with all his heart and leaned not on his own understanding and went forth and came seeing. We servants of God will do likewise. Knowing both the person and the power of the Son of God, we will go through all kinds of danger to help our neighbour; yea through a hostile crowd that would put an end to us. We will rely solely on the Lord to uphold us at all times and deliver us out of all persecutions. We will stop and stoop to minister to others in need and in so doing poor souls will sense our genuine concern and care for them and will be touched to open their hearts to us and will accept all that we have to tell them. We will then exhort, comfort and charge them to do right, and seek to be reconciled unto God. What joy it is to see one who was blind coming to see and believe on the Son of God. He that concerns himself with doing good to others, will not concern himself with the evil others do him, and so he will not be easily provoked.

Our Lord could not be provoked, even though His own slung false accusations at Him saying – "He casteth out devils through Belzebub" Lk.11:15, and that must have hurt, but oh how it must have pierced His heart when they said "we be not born of fornication," John 8:41 inferring that He was born out off wedlock. Yet, He did not retaliate. He did not return evil for evil, but love restrained Him from reacting with harsh words, and He remained cool, calm, collected and in complete control, responded with words savoured with grace. Now we servants of God are not exempt from being provoked, for they that know us will resurrect from the past some old skeletons which they will sling at us to hurt. We will not treat evil with evil. We will not lose our temper, but we will remain in control of our emotions and feelings, and will keep our minds on our business, seeking to steer souls to a knowledge of the goodness of God, and will deal graciously with all. The servant of God that loves his neighbour, and is not easily provoked, will not do him evil, neither does he think evil of him, but would rather see him changed for good.

Our Lord thought no evil of any one. He did not think evil of the woman caught in adultery or of those that caught her or those that accused her. Instead of pointing the finger of condemnation at any, He pointed his finger to the ground and wrote as though He heard nothing. Wisely, He stooped to consider the accusations and the accused and the accusers, and then stood up to use the word of God to judge and condemn them that commiteth sin, and challenge the accused to go sin no more. So, it is with we servants of God, we know that in times past we were as others, but we also know that God loved us and was merciful to us and forgave us our sins and the evil that we had done, so we must be moved with compassion, show mercy and consider the one with whom we speak and not condemn him for being evil, but stand up to challenge him to sin no more and repent and be converted to doing right. We no longer rejoice in iniquity but instead we love to do right and we seek to do it the right way.

Our Lord loved righteousness and rejoiced not in iniquity, for there was no evil in His heart. He could rejoice in saying – "the prince of this world cometh and hath nothing in Me." John 14:30. The Holy Spirit could rejoice at leading Him into the wilderness knowing, that He could not be tempted of evil. He rejoices at every son of God purposing within his heart to do no evil. God, the Father loveth righteousness and loved to see the Son doing right and rejoiced to see Him loving the unlovable, cleansing lepers, touching the untouchables, casting out demons, taming the untamable, making the blind to see, the lame to walk and raising the dead. We servants of God, will love righteousness and thirst after righteousness, and our lives will be filled with opportunities to do that which is right. We will rejoice in knowing what is right. We will rejoice in the truth, for it shows us what is right and sets us free from any doubt as to what we should do. We know this is the way and to walk in it. It sets us free from being confounded and confused. It sets us free to trust the Lord God with all our hearts, and since the Lord has set us free, we are free indeed. We are free, with authority from his Lord, to bear witness to the truth, and so we will declare the truth at all times.

Our Lord loved the truth. He was true and faithful and bore witness to the truth at all times. He did not compromise the truth to suit his hearers or withhold it to avoid hostility. It did not suit His hearers to hear our Lord tell them the truth saying – "ye are of your father the devil and the deeds of your father you do." John 8:44.

When a hostile crowd came to arrest Him, He knowing all things that should come upon Him, went forth, and said unto them, "Whom seek ye?" They answered Him, "Jesus of Nazareth". The Lord Jesus said unto them, "I Am." The truth that He was God and Jesus, set them back so that they fell to the ground. Likewise, we sons of God love the truth and we will not compromise it to suit anyone. We show people that they are bound to sin and bound to the power of satan and that they are bound to be punished in the lake that burneth with fire. The people don't like it. It doesn't suit them. It suits them to think that they are good and that they are going to heaven. We tell them the truth, because we love them. When they question us saying *who are you ?* We don't withhold the truth to avoid hostility, we gladly answer saying - *we are Ambassadors for Christ that come unto you to show you the need to be reconciled to God.* That takes them back. Nevertheless we are willing to suffer for our Lord, for what is right and for the truth of what is right. There are times when it troubles us to tell one that which he does not like to hear, but to hold back the truth to avoid hurting one's feelings is not doing that which is good and right. Love seeks to do good, and it is good to warn of the truth of danger, and it is not good to withhold the truth. The truth may shock and shake one momentarily, but it will not hurt and harm one permanently. Only love for our Lord and the truth and our neighbours will move us to bear all things in order that we might bear good tidings to those in need.

Our Lord bore all things, in bearing witness to the truth. He could say – "because for thy sake I have borne reproach, shame hath covered my face and the reproach of those that reproached thee are fallen on me." Psalm 69:7-9. Yes, He bore the shame, scorn, and sarcasm that sinners could sling at Him, and we who would be fishers of men must follow Him and likewise bear the slings and arrows of outrageous fortune. We do so rejoicing that we have been counted worthy to suffer shame for His name, and we know that the truth we have declared is the word of God, and it will not return unto Him void, but will accomplish that which He doth please and shall prosper whereto it is sent. We know that "God will have all saved and come unto the knowledge of the truth."1Tim.2:4. We know the truth that "all things work together for good to them that love God to them that are called according to his purpose." Rom.8:28. Knowing and accepting these truths, we go forth, believing all things.

Our Lord believed all things; He believed "the things which are impossible with man are possible with God" Lk.18:27. He believed that man without Him can do nothing. We, likewise believe that which is impossible with man is possible with God, and that God can change man which is impossible for man to do, and that without Him we can do nothing, for we are all sinners bent on doing wrong. In love for all sinners whether chief or not, we know that all can be saved and we believe that all can be saved and so we go forth to show the truth of salvation to all and we know that the Holy Spirit will strive with them that they may accept the truth. In love for them we hope and pray that they will wisely accept the truth, and be made wise unto salvation.

Our Lord hoped all things; He hoped that all that the Father gave Him would not be lost. He crossed a cruel sea in the hope of taming one who was untameable. There are those whom we know, trust and love, and they appear to be so set in their ways that their impenitent hearts are so hard that they will not repent and they will not accept the way of salvation, and there are those who are so religious and love their church but not the truth, and we wonder if ever they shall be saved. Their situation seems hopeless. There seems to be no hope for them, yet in love for them we hope against hope. We hope that when God sets them aside to make known unto them the truth that they will respond by accepting it. With patience of hope and in love for them we labour in prayer for them, and we would endure a sea of trouble to woo and win them. The servant of God will endure all things for the joy of seeing those he loves brought into relationship with God. He will follow the Lord, who endured all things for the joy of providing for man's reconciliation unto God.

Our Lord endured all things, the shame, the scorn and reproaches of man. He endured the contradiction of sinners against Himself, yet for the joy that was set before Him, He set His face as a flint to Calvary. He endured many things of the religious hierarchy who for envy had Him delivered to be judged, condemned and crucified. When they had brought Him to the place which is called Golgotha that is to say - a place of a skull, "they gave Him vinegar mingled with gall; when He had tasted, He would not drink."Math.27:34. It being the third hour they crucified Him.

In love for all that know not what they do, He prayed saying – "Father forgive them."Lk.23;34. In love for one who repented and would have Him rule over him, He assured him saying - "*today thou shalt be with Me in paradise*" *Lk.23:43*. In love for His mother, He provided for her immediate welfare. It was the sixth hour, and there was a darkness over all the earth until the ninth hour. During those three hours, God being Holy, spared nor His Son, and had to forsake Him whilst he bore the sin of the world. But in love He spared the world from seeing the suffering of the Son of God as He bore the punishment in full for the sin of the world. Our Lord cried out saying – "I thirst." John 19:28. The people, thinking they were doing Him a favor offered Him vinegar. He graciously did not disappoint and received it.

Now, He was not seeking a favour from man, but was expressing the extreme agony of His suffering as He was doing man the greatest favour possible in providing for his redemption, reconciliation, salvation and eternal blessing. Six hours earlier they offered Him vinegar. He would not drink, for it was mingled with gall. Herein, one can search the deep things of God and find the perfect love of God and the sovereignty of God in rendering to nought the devil's most subtle trick to undermine the Atoning work of our Lord Jesus Christ.

This cup that man offered our Lord contained vinegar mingled with gall, rendering it a stupefying mix that would have defiled Him. For it would have been absorbed into the blood stream and corrupted it and circulated to the brain to kill off cells. The smallest amount would have killed off one brain cell and marred Him physically and rendered Him imperfect, and His offering would have been imperfect and thus unacceptable to God.

It would also have marred Him mentally and rendered Him insensitive to pain and thus reduced His suffering in the time determined, and He would have required more time to bear the punishment in full for the sin of the world, by which time the Roman soldiers would have had to brake His legs to ensure death.

This would have refuted the prophetic word of God "that a bone of Him shall not be broken." John 19:36. It would have rendered His suffering insufficient to satisfy Divine Justice. It would have robbed Him of the right to lay down His life and removed the proof of His love.

This mix would have marred Him spiritually, for it would have rendered His love imperfect, and He would not have been perfectly obedient. He would not have been obedient unto death. That would not have pleased God the father, but would have pleased Satan who would have man call Him to come down from the cross, and He would have come down, for only perfect love could have kept Him on the cross.

Thus, we would have had no substitute to sacrifice, no saviour, no salvation.

Our Lord, being holy He was without blemish. There was nothing that defileth in Him and nothing that defileth could enter Him and mar His perfect love. We can thank and praise our Lord, that He did not accept the cup that man offered Him, but instead accepted the cup that God the Father gave Him, and on the cross He was the Lamb of God without blemish and without spot, and He was as sensitive as the day the woman touched the hem of His garment, and in perfect love for God the Father He was obedient unto death, even the death of the cross, and in perfect love for man, he bore the iniquity of us all, remained on the cross, and bore the punishment in full for the sin of the world. When He knowing He had consumed all the wrath of God against the sin of the world, and paid in full the price of man's redemption He in triumph cried out – "It is finished." John 19:30. Then He gave up the ghost that He might taste death for all. One of the soldiers with a spear pierced his side, and forthwith came there out blood and water. Herein is the proof of His death and proof of the greatness of His love.

Our Lord is worthy to receive glory, honour and power for He being holy, harmless, undefiled, separate from sinners, He is perfect, and was the perfect substitute that offered Himself the perfect sacrifice that did perfectly satisfy divine justice, did perfectly appease the wrath of God and did make perfect atonement for man with God and perfectly please God. God showed

His pleasure by raising him from the dead, exalting Him to the right hand of God, and giving Him a name that is above every name that at the name of Jesus every knee shall bow and every tongue confess that Jesus Christ is Lord to the glory of God the Father.

Truly, our Lord endured all the wrath of man for the cause of righteousness and endured all the wrath of God against the sin of the world in order to provide for man's reconciliation and redemption. We, who have been delivered from being bound to the power of sin and bound to the power of satan and bound for hades and the lake of fire, we would follow Him and be like Him in this world, and endure all things for His name and also for the blessing of our neighbour.

In love for righteousness our Lord thirsted after righteousness and suffered for the cause of righteousness, and in love for man He thirsted as He suffered in doing him the greatest favour possible. Our Lord, loved His disciples unto the end of His time in the flesh, and arose from the dead still loving them and in love for Peter and thirsting for his love, He immediately enquired of him, saying - 'lovest thou Me." John 21:16. Our Lord is alive for evermore, still loving those He has redeemed unto God with His blood, and He is still thirsting for the love of our redeemed hearts. *Lovest thou Him?* His love never faileth, neither should our love for Him fail. Love stoops to conquer and never fails, and with this assurance we go forth as coworkers together with our Lord to woo and win the unrighteous to righteousness.

# The Right Mode of Righteousness

God is righteous and doeth right, and God did right in creating man, and since the beginning God has been doing right to man. God did right in providing for the first man's reconciliation unto God after he had sinned and separated himself from God. God did right in having righteousness preached by Noah for 120 yrs. unto a world of unrighteous people.

God did right in imputing righteousness unto Abraham the moment he believed God, and God did right in setting aside the descendants of Israel as his earthly people, and by his righteous dealings with them He did manifest His righteousness to the nations. After the first generation of Israel, there arose another generation which knew not the Lord nor yet the works which He had done for them. They forsook the God of their fathers, which brought them out of the land of Egypt, and they followed the gods of the peoples that were round about them, and bowed themselves unto them, and provoked the Lord to anger. Pride closed their heart so that they did not want to hear. They rejected knowledge of God; they rejected God and turned to idols. In turn God rejected them, but not until they finally rejected the Son and crucified Him and persecuted his servants. Nevertheless, God has not rejected them forever.

God then turned to take out of the nations a people for his name, that they might be the righteousness of God bearing witness to the righteousness of God to and through them to a world of unrighteous people. This ministration of righteousness is by the right means of the Spirit of God operating through the people of God individually and collectively; working in harmony with the Holy Spirit in the unity of the Spirit and in obedience to the Spirit. It is the mode of operation of the Spirit of God in the dispensation of the Spirit of God. It is **the right mode of righteousness**. Accordingly the Spirit gives spiritual gifts to every man, dividing severally as He wills. So that we are all workers together with our Lord in the ministry of righteousness. We being many are one body in Christ and every one members one of another.

Having then gifts differing according to the grace that is given us we are each responsible for exercising our gift and engaging in the ministry. There must be no shirking our responsibility and leaving it to others, and no securing total ministry by one man, and no separating from the assembly to exercise one's gift elsewhere. Such free lance and one-man ministries are not in the mind of God, though they be in the minds of men; they are not scriptural. God's people are not independent, but interdependent; depending on one another for support, encouragement and cooperation so that united we stand.

God has purposed to minister righteousness to and through His heavenly people as they journey homeward through this world. Each and every child of God bears his own individual testimony to the righteousness of God. Subsequently a collection of God's people will bear a collective testimony to the righteousness of God. Such an assembly of believers is the temple of God the Holy Spirit and is comprised of temples not made with hands. It is founded, formed, and fashioned according to the mind, and will of God, as revealed in the word of God, which is law unto the children of God. Such an assembly is a building of people made righteous, doing right. It is a building of righteousness, a righteous building. It is the Lord God who builds the house, it is He who does that which is good and right, and it is He who is worthy of all praise, honour, and glory, and not his people. It is He, who is counted worthy of more glory than the servant, in as much as He who hath built the house hath more honour than the house of which we form part. It is the duty of each and every child of God to build righteousness into that building and thus build up the testimony. Each of us must purpose within our hearts to do right at all times, by the right means, for the right motive, and in the right manner. This is our responsibility. To this end were we converted. The Holy Spirit having sanctified each of us unto belief of the truth of salvation will further sanctify us unto belief of the truth of consecration, when by baptism in the public place we declare the purpose of our hearts to do right at all times. By total immersion we declare how we purpose to do right at all times - by dying to self, and alive unto God. Just as it pleased God the Father to see His only begotten Son declaring his purpose to fulfil all righteousness so also it pleases the Father to see each and every adopted son do likewise.

The Lord will order the steps of a righteous man and lead him aright in the ways of righteousness. In order to do so He must firstly separate him from evil and then lead him into all truth of what is right. God the Holy Spirit will lead him through the wilderness of religious confusion to humble him and prove him, and know what is in his heart, whether it be his desire to do right. Then He will lead him into the truth of gathering unto our Lord; according to the mind and will of our Lord as taught by the Apostles. The Holy Spirit will exercise him, even strive with him to accept the truth by joining those of like mind who seek to please God and do right, and daily they shall search the scriptures whether things be so.

They that steadfastly agree in the apostles doctrine will continue in fellowship one with another, walking in the light of God's word and walking worthy of the Lord unto all pleasing, walking worthy of the vocation to which they are called with all lowliness and meekness, with long suffering forbearing one another in love endeavouring to keep the unity of the Spirit in the bond of peace. Oh, how good and pleasant for brethren to dwell together in unity. But, oh how pleasing to God, for it is there that God's honour dwelleth, and it is there that

God commands the blessing. It is there that the Lord deigns to meet with his people; to control their affairs, to direct them aright, to protect them from all wrong, to feed and sustain them along the way, and preserve them. This work, our Lord does himself through his Spirit indwelling each and every child of God. Our Lord does not delegate this work to man. For a man to think more highly of himself than he should and presume that God ministers solely through him to the edification of the saints, he doth err not knowing the scriptures, and doth sin. It is contrary to the mind and will of God as ordered by our Lord and taught by the apostles.

The apostle Paul taught against such ministry. - see Romans 12:4-10, and 1Cor.14:29-34. The apostle John warned against such ministry. see 3John. The apostle Peter forbids such ministry. see 1Peter5:3. Such ministry of lording it over God's heritage practised by any person whether padre, priest, parson, or pastor is clerisy. It is evil and God hates it for

1 - It denies Lordship to the lord God
2 - It denies Sovereignty to the Spirit of God
3 - It denies Priesthood to the priests of God
4 - It replaces real and true worship with ritualism
5 - It prohibits the free exercise of gift
6 - It confines administration of ordinances to a few
7 - It causes saints to be lazy as to searching the scriptures

8 - It stunts growth in the knowledge of the truth and arrests edification.

9 - It provides the ground for untruth and it's propagation.

10 - It presents a way that is unsafe and leads to woe.

11 - It puffs up man to make unreasonable claims.

12 - It leads to the pleasing of, but not to the perfecting of the saints.

Clerisy is the vain imagining of man. It is of the flesh, founded, formed, and framed by the wisdom and will of man around man, for man. It is all vanity. Such a foundation is not of God, and will not stand the test of time. "Nevertheless, the foundation of God standeth sure, having this seal the Lord knoweth them that are His. And, Let every one that nameth the name of Christ depart from iniquity." 2Tim.2:19.

The child of God should depart from places where they would teach and practice unsound doctrine that deny the character of God. He should also flee from places where the brethren walk not in the light of God's word 2Cor.6:14-18. Wherefore the child of God must come out from among them and be separate. Having separated from all that is evil and all that pleaseth not God, he will "seek after righteousness, faith, love, and peace with all that call on the Lord out off a pure heart." 2Tim.2:19-22. He will seek the place where God's honor dwelleth. That could be a local assembly. It is there that he can get rooted in the truth, and grow in the knowledge of the truth - for it is the ground of truth.

It is also the pillar of truth from which he can declare the truth of the righteousness of God. It is there he can fellowship with those of like mind in the gospel, seeking to woo and win others to doing right. Daily in the public place, and from house to house they will cease not to teach and preach Jesus Christ. Knowing the fear of the Lord, we persuade all. This fear of displeasing the Lord compels us to persuade all men, but the love of Christ for us constrains us to go. Our Lord said – "if you love me keep my commandments." John 14:15.

As living stones of faith bonded together with love they will come together into one place on the first day of the week to remember our Lord in the breaking of the bread and the drinking of the wine. As a spiritual house, an holy priesthood they will offer up spiritual sacrifices acceptable to God by Jesus Christ. All the brethren may, one by one speak forth the praises of Him who hath called them out off darkness into his marvellous light. "To offer the sacrifice of praise to God continually that is the fruit of our lips giving thanks to His name, and to do good and communicate forget not - for with such sacrifices God is well pleased." Heb.15:15-16. . These sacrifices follow the divine order observed throughout the volume of the book, namely that worship precedes service. When the remnant of Israel returned from captivity to build the temple as recorded in Ezra 3:3-7, they built the altar of the God of Israel and "from the first day of the $7^{th}$.month began they to offer burnt offerings unto the Lord, but the foundation of the temple of the Lord was not yet laid." God's earthly people worshipped God before they began to work, and God's heavenly people must learn from them, for these things were written aforetime for our learning. The setting aside of this order can lead to failure.

Much emphasis is laid on serving the Lord, and quite rightly so, but it must be done as ordered by God. The young convert is encouraged to get involved in witnessing, in giving his testimony, and giving out tracts. But few are encouraged to get to know, and trust, and love the Lord, and to express that love in word, that is worship. "Now we know that God heareth not sinners, but if any man be a worshipper of God and doeth His will, him He heareth." John 9:31. This is a great truth. Many would claim to worship God, yet they abide in fellowships where they are hindered from worshipping God in spirit and in truth. Some imagine that singing hymns accompanied by sweet sounds of an organ or piano is worship. They do so in ignorance. God's earthly people may use instruments in their worship but not God's heavenly people. "God who made the world and all things in it, seeing that He is Lord of heaven and earth, dwelleth not in temples made with hands, neither is worshipped with men's hands, as though He needed anything, seeing He giveth to all life, and breath, and all things." Acts 17:24,25. God needs not that which is made by man's hands to worship Him. They that worship outside the place appointed by God, do not the will of God and God will not hear them.

The new convert, in his eagerness to serve, will seek every opportunity to do so, and having mounted the platform to relate the story of his conversion he will seek to learn to preach. The flesh will lead him forth and will not only lift him up onto more platforms but will lift him up to think more highly of himself, and to imagine that he is the Lord's gift to the church. It will not lead him forth to lift his hand to knock doors, which the true evangelist must do in order to learn the mastery of his ministry. For it is there that he will suffer many knocks that he must need, in order to knock the pride out of him. It is there that he will learn how to deal with souls sensitively and tenderly even as a nurse cherisheth her children; so being affectionately desirous of them he is willing to impart unto them not only the gospel of God, but also his own self. It is there that the evangelist will learn to show a man that he is a sinner, rather than tell him. Firstly he has no right to tell a man that he is a sinner, and secondly he'd be wise not to do so. He dare not look into the eyes of a giant and tell him that he is a sinner bound for the blackness of darkness, for he himself is bound for trouble and possible darkness, and may be flung to the ground and fed to the fowls of the air.

The servant of God has the right to show a man that he is a sinner in need of a savour, and then tell him the good news of the only savour of sinners. He must show in order to earn the right to tell, in other words, he must teach in order to preach. This is another divine order that must be observed, as it was in apostolic times when the disciples ceased not to teach and to preach Jesus Christ in the temple and from house to house.

In modern times the vast majority of those engaged in evangelism have ceased to teach, but ceased not to preach. This they do from the high and lofty position of a platform; far from the hearer and far from harm, but not far from the praise of man. They have ceased to evangelise from house to house. The nearest a preacher gets to a sinner is to invite him to come to hear him tell him that which he feared to tell him on his door step.

The child of God who gets his priorities right will give the Lord, His rightful place in his life. He will spend much time revelling in the love of our Lord for himself and others and he will grow in love for the Lord, and express it in word which is worship and in deed which is service. He will go forth to reveal the love of the Lord to others. It has been well said - 'revelling in the love of the Lord makes easy the revealing the love of the Lord'. The greatest occupation available to man is to be occupied with God; worshipping and serving Him. The greatest privilege afforded man is to worship God, and the greatest responsibility entrusted man is to serve God. The child of God should be daily occupied with the greatness and goodness of God. He should take time to get alone with God, and the Spirit of God will take of the things of the Lord and show them unto him. Then on the Lord's day the Holy Spirit will exercise the child of God to offer the sacrifice of praise to God, and bring to remembrance those things that He showed him. With such a sacrifice, God is well pleased.

To do good and to communicate is another sacrifice with which God is well pleased. Now the greatest good the child of God can do is to communicate the goodness and greatness of God. This requires sacrificing much time to get alone with God in order to prepare to do that which is good and right. To do right is the birth right of every child of God, for only he has the right to tell others of that which he knows to be right, and only he has the enabling power of the Holy Spirit to do right.

Now, although we have been redeemed from a vain manner of conversation (living to please ourselves), and reconciled unto God as children of God and have the Holy Spirit indwelling us to save us from living to please ourselves, and enable us to live to please God, yet there is within each of us that would cause us to fail. Within each of us abides that old nature of wanting to please ourselves. This desire must be put to death daily. If not, it will to take control, and instead of decreasing that the Lord might increase, the reverse takes place. Self will seek to establish itself; for it wants to be a cut above the rest, and will not rest until it cuts down those above it. Such will find fault with those that have the rule over them. They will find fault with their ministry, motives, manner, and means. They cannot find fault with their gift. They will not find fault with the simple sheep but will seek to separate them from the flock to share their findings. Separating the flock pleases Satan, but not the chief shepherd. Sowing discord among brethren does not please God - for he that does so is an abomination unto God. c/f Prov.6:19.

The Spirit of God through the word of God beseeches the children of God to "mark them that cause divisions and offences contrary to the doctrine which ye have learned, and avoid them." Rom.16:17. When the child of God falls for the devices of the devil, he fails God. He falls from fellowship with God the Father, the Son of God, and the people of God. He no longer walks worthy of our Lord unto all pleasing. His steps are no longer ordered by the Lord. He may take that dreadful step away from the assembly and seek to establish himself in another. To leave a lawful assembly into which the Lord has lead one is not only turning one's back on God's people, but also on God. He is forsaking God's way in order to have his own way. He will learn the hard way, that the power and wrath of God is against all them who forsake Him.

Naomi had to learn that lesson. She went out full of the knowledge of the place where God promised blessing; full of blame, for she did not oppose her husband's decision, and did not return when her husband died. She was full of self-confidence, that she could provide for her sons, and fully aware of God's injunction against intermarriage with the nations. Naomi went out full, yes full of self, and lost her husband, her sons, all that she lived for. She had nothing left, her heart was broken, and would have abided in that state, except for the love of the Lord, who took pity upon her, and brought her back home again - but empty. Truly the Almighty had to deal bitterly with her in order to break down her stubborn self will and make her humble so that He could bless her. She had to learn the hard and bitter way.

So it is with every child of God who feeds on pride and in the fulness thereof goes out from the people of God. He would do well to note that the Lord will bring him back in His time, not the backslider's time, and that he will be brought back empty. Time will manifest if he be a son of God. If he be a son he would be wise to humble himself now under the mighty hand of God, that He may bring him back and exalt him in due time. On the other hand he may continue in strained fellowship with the brethren. In order to preserve the testimony of the local assembly God will chasten that child of God that He might restore him. If he be without chastisement, he is not a son, and God will have to purge him out. If he be a son then the Holy Spirit will convict him of wrong doing, and prompt him to consider his ways. He must realize that the way he has been living is not right and the wrong he has done is not only against God's people but is first and foremost against God. He must reconsider the way he wants to go in the future. Is he going to live to please God or is he going to pass the time of his sojourn here living to please himself; taking lightly the word of God, not taking earnest heed to the things which he has heard, hoping he will make it softly and safely through the night into blessing. He would do well to realize that salvation is not only from eternal punishment, but from sinning against God and doing evil to others, and from the evil that the devil and the powers of evil would do him through man and otherwise.

Wandering irresponsibly, the child of God gropeth at noonday as the blind gropeth in darkness, and he shall not prosper in his ways, he shall only be oppressed and spoiled evermore, and no man shall save him, for he offers himself prey to the devil, "who as a roaring lion walketh about seeking whom he may devour." 1Pet.5:8. How shall he escape if he neglects so great salvation? - there is no escape!! He must consider the end of the journey. Will he have an abundant entrance into the presence of God ?

His entrance will be a bitter-sweet one; for it will be sweet to know that his spirit is safe at last. But it will be bitter to inwardly digest that he received not, the gracious greeting from our Lord – "well done my good and faithful servant" and received no reward. Our Lord will not tell lies, and call a child of God a good and faithful servant if he has not served God and faithfully done good, nor will He reward him for deeds done in the flesh; for all his righteousnesses are as filthy rags. He must consider God's way. He would do well to examine himself, whether he be in the faith, prove his own self and know that Jesus Christ is in him or not. He should examine the cause of his departure, resolve within his heart to put things right and get right with God. Then confess his sins and request forgiveness. God who is faithful and just will forgive him his sins and cleanse him of all unrighteousness. He will depart from the place of the Holy rejoicing that he has been restored to fellowship with God and the Son, and go forth to be reunited with his brethren. Together, they will be of one mind humbly wanting to live to please God and do right.

Living to please God characterises the child of God. and he that abides not in living to please God is a strange child and should be strangely sobered on reading the words of our Lord – "not every one that saith unto me Lord, Lord shall enter the kingdom of heaven, but they that doeth the will of my Father who art in heaven." Math.7:21. The true child of God rejoices to read the words of Peter – "for as much as ye know that ye were not redeemed with corruptible things, silver and gold, from your vain conversation, received by tradition from your fathers; but with the precious blood of Christ, as a lamb without blemish and without spot, who verily was fore-ordained before the foundation of the world, but was manifest in these last times for you, who by him do believe in God, that raised him up from the dead, and gave him glory; that your faith and hope might be in God. Seeing ye have purified your souls in obeying the truth through the Spirit unto unfeigned love of the brethren; love one another with a pure heart fervently." 1Pet.1:18.

We who were no people are now the people of God. We have been redeemed from the vain manner of living to please ourselves. We have been reconciled unto God. We should walk worthy of our Lord unto all pleasing. We ought to follow our Lord with all our hearts and not live to please ourselves, but let everyone of us please his neighbour for good to edification.

Now the world will not understand us, but will see our good works and our love for the brethren and know that we are the children of God. They will despise, revile, and reject us; yet we should bear reproach for the Father's sake, just as our Lord, and like our Lord we should have a zeal for the house of God, the collective testimony of God's people that assemble lawfully in our locality. For it is founded on God the Son, formed by God the Holy Spirit, and fashioned by God the Father, all for the glory of our God. We should want to see everyone of our brethren walk in the truth and grow in righteousness, for the glory of God. We should want to see every creature won to doing right and pleasing God, for their own welfare and for the glory of God.

There shall be opposition. There always has been opposition to work of God. When the Jewish remnant returned from captivity in Babylon to build the house of God (the temple) there was much opposition. It is recorded in Haggai 1:9 - that God's house lay waste and every man ran unto his own house. Their interest in building a house for God waned but waxed towards building houses for themselves. They even used the materials that had been set aside for God's house. Their heart was not in the work. Opposition did not halt the work. Opposition will not halt the Lord's work; it may hinder the work. Only a half heart will halt the work!!

Now let us consider our ways. Is our whole heart in the work? Are we putting our best into the building up of the testimony of the assembly of which we form a part? Are we doing right at all times, offering the sacrifices of praise to God continually, and doing good and communicating the goodness of God continually? Or are we half-hearted in the work of our Lord doing right through us and building up the testimony to the righteousness of our God? If so, our interests are divided, and that presents a problem: for we can't serve two masters. For either we will hate the one and love the other or else we will hold to the one and despise the other. We cannot serve God and self. If our whole heart is not in the assembly then we have lost heart for God; we have lost the fear of displeasing God. We have left our first love. We love another. Another possesses our interest! It could be our house, our car, our money etc.

Such possessions can possess us: our time and talents and rob us of the privilege of meeting with God's people to worship, to pray, to study the scriptures, to teach and preach in the public place and from house to house. We shall miss such meetings, but shall not miss finding an excuse for being absent. A cold heart will find a thousand and one excuses for inactivity. Such find no favour with our Lord who looks upon the heart and knows that it is far from God. The desire of His heart is that we remember from whence we are fallen and repent and do our first works.

Let each of us examine our hearts and see if there be anything in us that would mar our love for the Lord, who is the head of the body; the Church, who is the beginning; the first born from the dead, that in all things He might have the preeminence. The Lord God must have the preeminent place in our hearts. When

He has His rightful place, then all will be right. He will work all things together for good to us that love Him. He will take us forth as workers together with Him to do that which is good and right and to preach the gospel to every creature.

# The Right Message of Righteousness

The child of God that is filled by the Spirit will love the Lord God and will also love his neighbour. He will love to do him good and communicate to him the goodness of God. He will follow after that which is spiritual that he may prophecy. He will speak of that which he knows, and testify of that which he has seen. He will go forth to woo and win the unrighteous to righteousness. He will declare the righteousness of God.

God did that which is good and right in creating the heavens and earth and all that is therein, for "He saw everything that He had made and behold it was very good" Gen.1:31. God created man to live in loving fellowship with Himself as sons of God forever conformed to the image of His only begotten Son the Lord Jesus Christ, who is perfect. Accordingly God created man in His own likeness, with an intellect, a conscience, and a free will that man may will to become a child of God. He does not impose a relationship on any one. God does right in sustaining His creation "in giving us rain from heaven, and fruitful seasons, filling man's heart with food and gladness" Acts 14:17. God is right in requiring that his creation do right, and do no wrong. God did right in making known unto man that which is not right, by laying down the law of the ten commandments. The law does not tell man what is right nor does it enable him to do what is right and please God. In this the law is weak through the flesh being strong in desire to please self rather than God.

Man being born separated from God, lacks the God given desire to please God, and so he does that which comes naturally; he lives to please himself. Lacking the desire to please God, he does not seek after God to know God's will, and being separated from God he lacks the power to do the will of God. So he is bound to do that which is contrary to will of God. That is sin and displeases God unto wrath, for each and every time a person sins against God, he does wrong (evil) to someone; even if it be himself. "As it is written there is none righteous, no, not one. There is none that understandeth, there is none that seeketh after God. They are all gone out off the way, they are altogether become unprofitable; there is none that doeth good, no, not one. Their throat is an open sepulchre, with their tongues they have used deceit; the poison of asps under their lips, whose mouth full of cursing and bitterness. Their feet swift to shed blood. Destruction and misery in their ways, and the way of peace have they not known. There is no fear of God before their eyes." Rom.3:10-18. Since all humans have this nature they do that which is sin and God has it recorded in Rom.3:23 – "all have sinned."

The devil knows the nature of man and he will tempt him to enjoy the pleasures of sin for a season, and man being separated from God and lacking divine power to resist the devil he is bound to do as the devil wills it. As it is written, man walks "according to the course of this world, according to the prince of the power of the air, the spirit that now worketh in the children of disobedience: Among whom also we all had our conversation in times past in the lusts of our flesh, fulfilling the desires of the flesh and of the mind; and were by nature the children of wrath, even as others." Ephes.2:2-3. Man is not only bound to sin, but he is bound also to the control of the devil, who will tempt him to sin against God and do evil to his fellow man. So the good that he would he does not and the evil that he would not he does. Likewise he will tempt others to sin against God and do him evil. So the way of peace and happiness he knows not. Such is the vanity of life. As man continues sinning, willfully and under the tempting of the devil, his life builds up in sinning against God and doing evil. He is also treasuring up unto "himself wrath against the day of wrath and the revelation of the righteous judgment of God, who will render to every man according to his deeds." Rom.2:5,6. God has declared, "the wages of sin is death" Rom.6:23, and has decreed in Isaiah 13:11, that He will *"punish the world for evil"*. Isa.13:11

The word of God makes it clear that "in flaming fire taking vengeance on them that know not God, and that obey not the gospel of our Lord Jesus Christ: Who shall be punished with everlasting destruction from the presence of the Lord, and from the glory of his power;" 2Thes.1:9,10. This punishment being everlasting, must be executed in eternity. He that has not obeyed the gospel shall stand before God at the great white throne, and be judged in righteousness, and then cast into the lake of fire, where God will render to every man according to his deeds. They that have committed many sins and did great evil shall be separated from God and great shall be their punishment and suffering. He that has committed less sin, and did less evil, even though he did much good shall be separated from God and shall be punished less. They shall each be able to say - *my punishment is greater than I can bear.*

To pass one's sojourn on this earth living to please self, not knowing the happiness of living to please God is all vanity. To die unchanged, unconverted, unredeemed, never to know happiness and spend eternity knowing the wrath of God is the vanity of vanities.

Since man is bound to sin against God and do evil, and bound to the control of the devil, and bound to be punished and bound for hell and the lake of fire, man needs someone to redeem him from living to please himself, and save him from sinning against God and doing evil and the punishment for doing evil.

What can man do to redeem himself from such a vain manner of living and reconcile himself unto God and save himself from further sinning against God and doing further evil ?

There is nothing man can do!

There is nobody can save him!

There is no body of people, such as a church body can save him; whether it be Moslem, Jewish, Roman Catholic, or Protestant.

Man is undone. There is no hope in man!!

But there is hope in God!!

God who created man knew that man would sin against Him and do evil.

God being just, will punish all that do evil, and did decree saying, "I will punish the world for evil." Isa.13:11.

God being love, so loved the world that "He will have all saved, and come unto the knowledge of the truth."

God being all wise, according to His infinite wisdom, did create His plan of salvation whereby He would punish sin, and pardon the sinner, and reconcile him unto God, and save him from living to please himself and the terrible consequences thereof.

God being righteous did right in sending His Son to be the saviour of the world, and to be the propitiation for sins of the whole world. c/f 1John 2:2.

God the Son did right in coming into this world to save sinners, to put away sin, and do the will of Him who sent him. Great was His entrance into this world, for an angel did herald the glad tidings saying – "unto you is born this day in the city of David a saviour, who is Christ the Lord" Lk.2:11, and with that angel a great multitude of the host of heaven praising God saying – "glory to God in the highest, and on earth peace, good will toward men." Lk.2;14 God who prepared Him a body and made of one blood all nations of peoples, made Him not of that blood, for His blood was His own. Only His blood was incorruptible, innocent and undefiled.

Whilst the birth of all humans is the beginning of their being, the birth of the Lord Jesus Christ was the entrance into a new mode of existence of one, who had no beginning, and who being in the beginning was with God and was God, and being in the form of God thought it not robbery to be equal with God: but made himself of no reputation, and took upon him the form of a servant, and was made in the likeness of men: and "being found in fashion as a man, He humbled himself, and became obedient unto death, even the death of the cross."Phil.2:6.

Through the miracle of the virgin birth He who is truly God became truly man. He ceased not to be God. He did not empty himself of his divine nature or attributes. He who in the beginning was the Word, was made flesh, and dwelt on this earth. He came into the world to manifest God in the flesh and to bring judgment to the nations. Without controversy great is the mystery of godliness: God manifest in the flesh. Of a truth it is written "no man hath seen God at any time; the only begotten Son, which is in the bosom of the Father, he hath declared Him." John1:18.

He being God, He is righteous and loveth righteousness and hateth iniquity, and did right in consecrating himself to fulfilling all righteousness, and that did please God the Father, for He declared – "this is my beloved Son, in whom I am well pleased" Math3:17. He did not hide righteousness within His heart, but went forth to declare righteousness, and the Holy Spirit lead Him as a servant into the wilderness to prove that He could not be tempted of evil, and permitted the devil to tempt Him under the most adverse conditions to act independent of the Father. But, he being holy there was no blemish in Him and did rightly say "the prince of this world cometh and hath nothing in me." John 14:30. He could not sin. He was the sinless servant that relied solely on God the Father to uphold Him at all times.

To Him was given all power that is in heaven and in earth and He used His power to supplicate the throne of God, for in the morning, "a great while before day He went forth, departed to a solitary place" Mk 1:35, and morning by morning the Father opened His ear. He was not rebellious; daily he was the Father's delight. He did not please himself, but did always those things that please the Father. He did not behave Himself unseemly; he did not cry out, lift up or cause His voice to be heard in the street. He did not thirst after position, power, and possessions, but He thirsted after righteousness, and went about healing all that were oppressed of the devil, and healing all manner of sicknesses and diseases. Our Lord sought not His own, and did right in seeking the welfare of others. Even though a hostile crowd took up stones to cast at him, He seeing a man who was blind from birth, stopped. He stooped down and made clay of the spittle and anointed the man's eyes, and said – "go wash in the pool of Siloam." John 9:7. The man obeyed went and washed and came seeing. When he felt the Master touch his eyes, his heart was touched and he trusted the Lord with all his heart, and leaned not on his own understanding. Blind eyes did not blind the blind man from seeing the love of the Lord Jesus Christ. He acknowledged the goodness of our Lord, for he testified saying "one thing I know, that, whereas I was blind, now I see," John 9:25, and he also knew "that since the world began was it not heard that any man opened the eyes of one that was born blind." John 9:32. Of a truth, this man had both seen the power and the person of the Son of God, and did believe. This man, like all had a need, but unlike most, he wanted to see. Of a truth, Jeremiah did say – "there is nothing too hard for thee," Jer.32:17, "heal me O Lord and I shall be healed save me O Lord and I shall be saved." Jer.17:14.

Our Lord being just, is no respecter of persons, and showed justice in His dealings with all peoples of all nations, and wants to do good to each and every human being. He desires to bring all into relationship with Himself and heal all of the old sinful nature and save all from the consquences thereof. Our Lord being affectionately desirous of all ceased not to do favours to all that would appreciate. But being all wise did right in withholding favours to each that He knew would not appreciate His goodness. He being sensitive to the infirmities of man, He was as gentle as a dove, even as a mother that cherisheth her children. He being all knowing, all wise, and all mighty, He was in full control of each and every situation. He did right at all times with a right mind, for the right motive, in the right manner (that becometh the Son of God). He lived a life of perfect righteousness.

This is the life that God requires of each and every human being, but all have come short, for all have sinned. His life in the flesh ended in Him doing that which was perfectly right, when He set His face as a flint to Calvary, to be made sin for us, He who knew no sin that we might be made the righteousness of God in Him. There He suffered for the cause of righteousness. He suffered at the hands of man. He gave His back to the smiters, His cheeks to them that would pluck off the hair, and hide not His face from shame or spitting, and offered Himself through the Eternal Spirit without spot unto God to put away sin. The Lord Jesus Christ, being holy, harmless, undefiled, separate from sinners, He is perfect and only He could be the perfect substitute, that could provide Himself the perfect sacrifice that could satisfy divine justice and appease God's wrath against the sin of the world. It "pleased the Lord to bruise Him" Isa.53:10, and He laid on Him the iniquities of us all. "He was wounded for our transgressions, bruised for our iniquities, the chastisement of our peace was upon Him and with his stripes we are healed." Isa53:5. "Christ suffered once for sins, the just for the unjust, that He might bring us to God." 1Pte.3:18. He was delivered for our offences, so that we could be delivered from the punishment for our offences.

When He knowing He had borne the punishment in full for the sin of the world, and satisfied divine justice, and appeased God's wrath against the sin of the world, and had made atonement for man with God, He in triumph cried out – **"It is finished"** John 19:30 Then He gave up the ghost that He might taste death for all.

God manifested His pleasure by raising the Christ from amongst the dead, exalting him a Prince and Saviour, and seating Him at the right hand of majesty on high, and "God gave Him a name that is above every name: that at the name of Jesus every knee should bow, of things in heaven, and things in earth, and things under the earth; and that every tongue should confess that Jesus Christ is Lord, to the glory of God the Father." Phil.2:9.

The Lord Jesus Christ is alive for ever more to save to the uttermost all that come unto God by Him seeing He ever liveth to make intercession for them. He is able and willing to save man from further sinning against God and doing further evil, and from further evil being done to him.

God in raising our Lord Jesus Christ from the dead declared in a most powerful and convincing way that Jesus Christ is the Son of God, justified the perfect righteousness of His life and death, vindicated the cause of righteousness, and assured man that God the judge of this world doeth right and shall judge the world in righteousness. Acts 17:31

God, being just is pleased to justify each and every sinner that accepts the atoning sacrifice of His Son, and accepts Him as Lord of his life. At that moment God justifies that believer from all things, "from which he could not be justified by the law of Moses." Acts 13:39. God puts him right with Himself, sees him as perfectly righteous as His Son for He is our righteousness, then He adopts him as a son. That is his standing before God. Because he is a son, God sends forth the Spirit of His Son into his heart.Gal.4:6. He is born again of the Spirit of God into the family of God, and given a new nature, the divine nature of wanting to live to please God the Father.

Now, although he stands before God as perfect and righteous, that is not his state of living, yet God would have him live up to his standing. Accordingly God will perfect that concerning His own. God, having put a man right with Himself would have him live right and do right and thus must save him from doing wrong. The Lord God will direct him aright, and by His Spirit enable him to do good and right and protect him from all evil and wrong. In order to do so, He must control his affections, his emotions, his thinking. his reasoning, his choosing, his will, his words, and his actions. He must be in complete control. He must be Lord of that person's life. If He is not Lord, He will not save him. He will not control man against his will.

The fact that the Lord Jesus Christ bore man's sins and the punishment in full for his sins, means that his sins have been already punished, and there is no need for them to be punished a second time. The Lord God has done man the greatest good in providing for his redemption from a vain manner of living, for his reconciliation unto God, for his salvation from the sinful nature and for his eternal blessing. Each human being has the right to choose, whether to accept the goodness of God or not. If one doesn't accept the goodness of the Lord God, then he must accept the punishment himself beyond the grave in the lake of fire. If one does accept the goodness of God, then he shall receive a pardon from the punishment that he rightly deserves for the wrong (evil) that he has done. He or she shall also be adopted into the family of God as a son of God, and redeemed from the vain conversation of living to please himself, and saved from the consequences thereof, and go forth to live to please his heavenly Father, now and throughout eternity.

It behoves man to perceive the goodness of God in providing for man's reconciliation, redemption and salvation. The goodness of God should move man to want to repent; to stop living to please himself, and turn to living to please God and do right.

It is right to punish a sinner that will not repent.

It is also right to pardon a sinner that will repent.

God is righteous, and doeth right, and wants to do right to each and every creature. He would have every one repent and believe the gospel, and come into relationship with Himself simply by accepting the great truth that "Christ Jesus also hath once suffered for sins, the just for the unjust, that He might bring us to God." 1Pet.3:18.

The Lord Jesus Christ would have every believer consecrate himself to doing right at all times by being baptized, and has given this assurance '"he that believeth and is baptized shall be saved" Mk.16:16. This means that every believer (child of God) that consecrates himself to doing right will be saved from doing evil. One should not misconstrue this scripture to mean that one must be baptized to become a believer (child of God).

He that believes on the Son hath everlasting life. He is a born again into the family of God. He who in times past was nobody is now a son of God. He is a new creature: old things are passed away; behold all things are become new. He has new desires. He now wants to do that which is good and right and communicate to others the goodness of God. He should seek to do it the right way.

This is his ministry and he should strive for the mastery of it. He is not crowned, except he strives to do it the right way that is - lawfully. He should seek a message from God. The Spirit of God will not disappoint and will give that child of God a right message, like unto that of the foregoing message.

This message I received not from man, nor was I taught by man, but the Spirit of God revealed it to me through the word of God. It is a clear, concise, yet comprehensive presentation of the truth of reconciliation and salvation. It is a message that is directed via the mind at the heart, which is the target of the soul winner. The message is intended to face the hearer with the bad news that he is a sinner condemned. Then show him the good news of the goodness of God in providing for his redemption, reconciliation, salvation and eternal blessing.

Both the bad and good news are absolutely necessary. The bad news is needed to show a sinner the vanity of living to please self. The good news is needed to convince him of the goodness of God and lead him to repentance toward God and faith toward our Lord Jesus Christ. To omit the bad news and concentrate on the good news, makes for a message that bypasses the mind and goes straight to the heart. Since it bypasses the pricks of conscience it bypasses the need for repentance and is easy to accept. It is a soft message that will woo a soul blindly into an unintelligent, profession, which is emotional, fleeting and false.

Souls that never repented, were never converted in the first place. They will return to the old ways. It is difficult to show them the error of their profession and face them with the need to repent. They that preach the soft gospel are guilty of not preaching the whole counsel of God regarding salvation and are guilty of misleading souls into false professions.

Just as there are those who preach a message that omits the bad news, there are those who preach a message that omits the good news. They concentrate on facing a soul with the hard facts of life that he is a sinner condemned. This hard gospel message goes as far as the mind, but fails to get down to the heart. Under concentrated pounding the soul is pressurized into submission and a false profession. To convince an unbeliever against his will he is one still. He will endure for a while, yet since it hath not taken root in his heart he will not stand in the day of trial. It is difficult for one to accept that which he has held back in unrighteousness.

They that preach the hard gospel are equally guilty of not preaching the whole counsel of God regarding salvation and of misleading souls into false professions. To mislead a soul into a false profession is a great evil. For the soul that falls away knows not whether he is an unbeliever in need of repentance, a backslider in need of restoration or an apostate that cannot be renewed to repentance. Only God knows his position.

The bad news is needed to break down the heart of the old man that wants to please self. The good news is needed to replace it with the heart of a new man that wants to please God. The preacher must not break a soul down, and leave him there. Oh no, he must lift him up to a better hope. Regrettably most hard gospel preaching concentrates and preponderates on judgment and warning of the wrath to come and leaves souls abiding in wrath. Such preachers not only leave sinners in the gutter of ruin without hope, but leave themselves gloating in that in that they have 'socked' it to them. They leave the brethren knowing they have pleased the old die-hards who recall preachers of bygone days warning sinners, - turn or burn. They definitely do not please our Lord, for such preachers fail to do good and communicate the goodness of God. They fail to realize that it is not the judgment of God that leadeth a sinner to repentance, but the goodness of God. Furthermore, in their haste to get a sinner to behold what lies below and before him they momentarily stop at the cross to declare that God has provided pardon for them. They fail to take time to show why our Lord must needs suffer, be slain and raised the third day. The preacher who spends little time at the cross will spend less or no time at the tomb to explain why the stone was rolled away. So the poor soul will not get the opportunity to see in, and see that He is risen, and is alive for evermore to save him to the uttermost, and that He is "Lord both of the dead and the living." Rom.14:9, and must needs be Lord of his life.

Preaching that confines salvation to that from eternal punishment and leaves out salvation from the power of sin and the power of satan, offers pardon from the punishment for sins, but no provision for the cessation of sin and doing further evil. It is natural and easy to accept a pardon, but it is not natural and easy to accept another person to rule over one's life, and so such preaching should open the flood gates for many to flow in, with none to follow Him.

Gospel preaching that offers pardon for sins and provision for the cessation of sin, requires one to accept both the work and person of the Lord Jesus Christ, and there shall be no flux of professors, but a small trickle of possessors of Him who will not be not ashamed to call them brethren, for they shall follow Him.

Both the soft and hard gospel messages focus on the effects of the problem and fail to focus on the source of the problem, that of the heart wanting to please self.

Bitter water comes from a bitter source (fountain) cf Math.12:35, Lk 6:45., Mk 7:23. One must change the source. When a certain woman had an issue of blood she reached out by faith and touched the hem of His garment, straightway the fountain of her blood was dried up. Our Lord went to the source of the problem. Likewise one must go to the source of the problem and seek to change the heart, the desire to live to please one's self. That is the heart of the problem, for out off the heart come evil.

The gospel preacher must preach man's ruined nature of wanting to live to please himself with the terrible consequences and God's remedy in a kinsman to redeem man from that vain manner of living and save him to the uttermost and enable him to live to please God. Man's responsibility is to want to change and trust the Son of God to heal and save him.

Let all things be done decently and in order, and so the message of the righteousness of God must be presented in an orderly manner, precept upon precept; here a little, there a little. Whether with stammering tongue or eloquence of speech, the message must be preached with boldness and plainness, not with enticing words of man's wisdom, but in the demonstration of the Spirit and of power.

It should be preached by the right method.

# The Right Method of Righteousness

God requires His people to do that which is good and right to each and every creature that one meets. Since it is God who does good and deigns to do so through His people, then each child of God should seek the Lord's preparation to do the good that he should. Each will go forth ready to speak a word in season to the broken hearted, to those held captive by sinful habits, to those that are blind to the truth, to those that are oppressed and to preach the gospel to the poor. God will lead that child of God to the one ordained to receive the goodness of God. He may meet and speak to many people that day, but will only be permitted to preach the gospel to the one prepared to hear it. To some he may speak words of comfort; to others he may speak words of encouragement; to some he might speak words of guidance. Nevertheless he will seek to do the greatest good and preach the gospel to each and every creature. This was the daily practice of the apostles, and they rejoiced at the privilege and were willing to suffer for His name and the cause of righteousness. Each of the twelve being filled with the Holy Spirit, only did so as allowed by God. They did not offend by trying to speak to those not prepared and set apart by the Holy Spirit.

This was the method used by Philip, see Acts 8:26-40. In obedience to the word of the Lord, Philip arose and went down to the Gaza desert: the most unlikely place to meet anyone. The Holy Spirit did not lead him in vain, for there he observed one of great authority with his entourage of servants and chariots, travelling down towards the south. The Spirit of God told him to go near and join himself to the chariot that carried the Ethiopian Eunuch. He did not tell him to preach to all the persons of the party in order to preach the gospel of peace and bring glad tidings to the one that He had ordained to hear the word of God that day, yea that hour. He lead him to the one that He had prepared, and at the right moment when he was reading the word of God. This meeting was all of God and for God. It was not convened by Philip, nor by the elders at Jerusalem, but by the Spirit of God. When the Holy Spirit convenes a meeting regarding faith in the Lord Jesus Christ, He prepares both His messenger and the hearer.

This was the method used by the apostle Paul to preach the Son of God among the heathen. He was bold in our God to speak unto the people the gospel of God, as he was allowed of God to be put in trust with the gospel, even so he spoke not as pleasing men, but God who trieth their hearts. He kept back nothing that was profitable, but showed the people and taught them publicly and from house to house, "testifying both to the

Jews and also to the Greeks, repentance toward God, and faith toward our Lord Jesus Christ" Acts 20:20,21.

This method requires the child of God to get up and go to those in need and bring glad tidings of good things and preach the gospel of peace. It requires the servant of God going to the lame those that cannot get up and go; to the blind that cannot see their way; to those that are deaf and cannot hear; to those that are afar off. It requires a debtor to the wise and unwise to go to meet face to face with one, a debtor to God, to confront him or her with the truth and confess the Lord Jesus Christ to be the one who can meet all their need. This method requires enduring the contradiction of sinners and suffering for the cause of righteousness. This method requires being filled with the Spirit, for only then can the child of God be free to be used as a coworker together with the Lord to do that which is good and right, giving no offence in any way.

This method that God uses to call out of the world a people unto His own name, the enemy feared would turn the world upside down, has turned the people of God off doing what is right the right way and turned them to another way, a softer way that avoids confrontation, contradiction and suffering. They have turned to that of staging the preaching of the gospel, whereby the preacher sets the time and place to his convenience. Such a method requires the lame, the blind, the deaf and those with physical weaknesses to get up and go to where the preacher is to be found. In the spiritual realm, if he be lame and bent in doing wrong and bowed down in shame and guilt and can in no wise stand upright for what is right, he will halt at the thought of going to a gospel meeting, for he will in no wise stand amongst the upright. If he be blind and doesn't want to see himself as a sinner he will not want to see his way to a gospel meeting. If he be a outcast of society he will not come near the camp, the hall or tent. If he be deaf and does not want to hear what others have to say, he will definitely not come to hear one tell him, he is a sinner going to hell. If he be dead in trespasses and sins and set in his ways, he will not rise up out of his sins and wrong doings and set himself toward a gospel meeting. Of a truth "there is none that seeketh after God" Rom.3:11 Realizing this truth the child of God must go.

To set up a meeting with one or more by choosing the time and place, and then shaping the conversation towards the gospel or the setting up of meetings in halls, tents or the open air for the preaching of the gospel, is all of man. Could it be all for man? The heart is deceitful, and man wants to make a name for himself. He will set the stage to put on a performance that he hopes will impress others. "For no man doeth any thing in secret, and he himself seeketh to be known openly". John 7:4. They that do so, will cite Peter's preaching on the day of Pentecost and Paul's preaching on Mars Hill as justification for this method of preaching. Now both occasions were the exception rather than the practice, for it is recorded that only once more did Peter preach to a large crowd, but with the eleven he ceased not to daily teach and preach Jesus Christ in the public place and from house to house. It is recorded that Paul preached the word of God in the synagogues at Salamis. He reasoned with the Jews as he did at Ephesus Acts 18:19. He definitely did not convene such meetings. But he definitely kept back nothing that was profitable but showed sinners and taught them publicly and from house to house, testifying both to the Jews and also the Greeks (gentiles), repentance toward God and faith toward our Lord Jesus Christ.

On the occasions that Paul and Peter preached to crowds of people, the people did not gather to hear the preaching of the word. The apostles did not set the time and place for the meeting. They had no foreknowledge that the Holy Spirit would convene a meeting for the preaching of the gospel, even though they had apostolic power (right). Yet today preachers claim that the Holy Spirit would have them convene series after series of gospel meetings. It is strange that the Holy Spirit does not exercise them to go preach the gospel from house to house.

Now God cannot be limited and can and has used such meetings to deal with souls. Nevertheless, it is not the method by which God will have His people do right in communicating the truth of the goodness of God, and by which sinners can be made wise unto salvation. God will have all men to be saved, and to come unto the knowledge of the truth 1Tim.2:4. How then shall they come unto the knowledge of the truth "How shall they believe in him of whom they have not heard? and how shall they hear without a preacher?

and how shall they preach, except they be sent ? as it is written - How beautiful are the feet of them that preach the gospel of peace, and bring glad tidings of good things" Rom.10:14,15. God by Sovereign grace will do each soul a favour that he or she does not deserve. God will present truth to each and every creature and He does it without one having to raise a finger, without one having to rise up and go anywhere, and without one having to be lead. "So then faith by hearing and hearing by the word of God" Rom.10:17. This is the work of God, "that ye believe on Him whom He hath sent." God will do His part by presenting truth to man, and man's part is to exercise his will in simply accepting the truth presented, that is believing. God does not impose His will on any one. He does not have His people force souls to accept the truth. He does not need a preacher to coerce one into accepting the truth by button-holing them and making altar calls. Man does not have to give account of himself unto man.

God will prepare and send a servant to the one He has ordained to hear the truth. The personal worker does not convene the meeting. He simply goes forth in faith seeking to do good to every creature knowing that the greatest good he can do, is to preach the gospel of the goodness of God. Sisters likewise are required to do good to their neighbour and like Philip's four daughters speak forth the word of God. Since there is no mention in the scriptures of them going from house to house preaching the gospel, one can assume that the Spirit of God being touched with the feeling of their infirmities as the weaker vessel would spare them from being shamefully treated.

God in order to send the truth to each and every creature, will order circumstances to convene a meeting between a servant and a sinner, regarding faith in Christ Jesus. The Spirit of God, having convened a meeting will use the word of God to convict the latter of his wrong doing; convince him that he needs a saviour and that the Lord Jesus Christ is the saviour he needs, and constrain him to accept the word and He who is the word incarnate. He does not need or want any improvisation from man. He does not need man to set the time and the place for Him to minister righteousness. Nor does He need to use music as the instrument of conveying truth. No need of soft wave notes to turn the key of one's heart and lull them into a shallow sentimental profession or hard rock to rock one into a rocky one.

The Holy Spirit needs no spectacle to do that which is spectacular. He does not need a preacher make a spectacle of himself by crying out to high heavens, and then crouching down to cast the finger of condemnation at his audience. Such performances may entertain and impress the saints, but they definitely fail to entreat the sinner to consider his ways other than his way out, and so he politely suffers such ostentatious orations until relieved on hearing the closing prayer. The saints that are easily impressed, will press you with that question you were hoping to avoid, by asking - *'didn't you enjoy that message?'*. So rather than offend, yet realizing you must not tell a lie, you muster all the resources of diplomacy and answer the question with the rhetorical question - *'you enjoyed it'.* The personal worker is sincere, true and faithful. He is for real, not given to acting, dramatics or such antics. It would be to his shame to behave in such an unseemly manner. If he were to put on such a performance in bringing glad tidings to one in need, in all bewilderment and amazement that one would lower his eyebrow and would rightly judge him saying - *thou art beside thyself; much preaching doth make thee mad.*

Then again, there is the preacher that is happy in having made a name for himself amongst the people of God; he will take liberty in his preaching, to jest or add a little humour. This light hearted approach to doing the Lord's work leads to taking lightly the word of God, and leads to many professions. But since the word is received by the way, the enemy can come along and snatch it away. The Holy Spirit warns against such jesting. Eph.5:4. He does not need one to humour souls into heaven.

The Holy Spirit does not prompt the preacher to call upon sinners at the close of a meeting to raise their hand, or raise themselves, or to come forward or sign cards. Nor does He need repeated calls to convince a sinner, but the carnal preacher needs to repeat his call in order to twist someone into a profession. and will justify repeated calling by saying - *'I feel there is someone in the hall tonight who is on the verge of making a decision, and needs further encouragement'*,- even a further six times; yea it is all of man. Or he may use another old arm twister - *I feel that there is some*

*one in the hall tonight who is on the verge of eternity'.*
Such stratagems are used to coerce souls into making
a profession marked by others but most of all marked
by the preacher.

The Holy Spirit does not use such devices, and
definitely does not have the servant of God indecently
shame sinners by asking all who are saved to stand up,
leaving all the unsaved seated and sorry they came to
such a sham. Such shenanigans are used by preachers,
that skip sensitivity to shame simple souls into a
salvation that is spurious.

The Holy Spirit needs no help from man in bringing
to remembrance truth. He needs not man to present
themes of truth under headings, all beginning with the
same letter. The canning of truth under 'B's, 'E's, 'A's,
'N's, and 'Ps' and 57 varieties of the same is concocted
in the mind of man, to convey to the mind of another
that this preacher is God's messenger in God's message.
He might convey this to some brethren, and con himself
into thinking that he has a message from God, for he
imagines that the Holy Spirit planned it so. In so doing
he only makes it obvious that he is not controlled by
the Spirit of God and has no message from God. He
definitely does not con the sinner, for he cares not
about alliteration; but worse still he does not convey
to him the fundamental truths concerning the Lord
Jesus Christ, for they will not fit into his canning. Such
Heinz preaching is a new way of conveying the Lord
Jesus Christ. It was not heard of in the early church. The
apostles never used it. It is all about the gospel, but not

the gospel, for it never gets to the heart of the matter. Heinz preaching is from the head of one to the head of another, and enjoyed by sermon tasters. In gospel preaching there are no sermons, no headings, other than for the heart. Gospel preaching is from the heart of a debtor to man to the heart of a debtor to God. The servant of God must preach from the heart, yes with all that in him is.

The heart will constrain him to take time to deliberately sow each seed of truth, and restrain him from rapidly running off all that is in his head to the hearer's head, hoping that some truth will settle, but in actual fact does not get time to settle and only unsettles the hearer, so that he will not hear further. Such rapid fire preachers fail to realize that the simple mind can only take in one truth at a time, and needs time to take it in, and inwardly digest it. He must preach the word of God, to be heard and understood, "for faith by hearing, and hearing the word of God." Rom.10:17. There are those who know this scripture, and take no thought, how or what they shall speak; presuming it shall be given in that same hour what they shall speak, and so they speak forth 'off the cuff' without a message from God, and they speak forth whatever scripture comes into their head, imagining that the Spirit of God is bringing to remembrance and giving them that which they should say. The Holy Spirit is not obligated to give them words at their convenience. Such preachers are unaware that they are committing the sin of presumption, and such preaching exempts the preacher from guiding the sinner into understanding what he hears and giving reasonable answers when questioned.

Staging the preaching of the gospel is the will of man and requires man setting the time and the place for the Holy Spirit to begin a good work. Whether it be in the open air, a hall, or a tent it requires an audience coming to a place designated by man and at a time appointed by man. This is the way of man. If souls are to find help there, they must find their way to that place or be brought there by man. The lost, the powerless, helpless and hopeless must get up and go to seek man that they might find God. Since it was started by man it will be performed by man. It is all of man and not of God. Man figures that the more who hear, the more will receive. The preacher can speak forth to crowds of people gathered to hear him and on all occasions preach the gospel to not one creature in need, not one that feareth God, not one prepared. In vain do they preach, for "there is none that seeketh after God, no, not one."Rom.3:11.

Human reasoning is no substitute for "the way of the Spirit, how the bones in the womb of her that is with child, even so thou knowest not the works of God that maketh all. In the morning sow thy seed, and in the evening withold not thine hand: for thou knowest not whether shall prosper, either this or that, or whether they both alike good." Ecc.11:5-6. If one who is sensitive to the leading of the Spirit be found doing so, then the still small voice will come unto him and say - *what doest thou here.* He will convict that servant of such vanity and take him aside to bring him to repentance and then prepare and lead him forth to the one in need, the one that feareth God, the one to whom God will send the word of salvation, the one that He has prepared for him to minister that day. This is the Scriptural method of communicating the goodness of God to a world that is without knowledge of God.

God had the disciples use this method to get the message to the uttermost part of the earth. They used it on the day of Pentecost, for it is recorded in Acts 2:4-14. "and they were all filled with the Holy Ghost, and began to speak with other tongues, as the Spirit gave them utterance. And there were dwelling at Jerusalem Jews, devout men, out of every nation under heaven. Now when this was noised abroad, the multitude came together, and were confounded, because that every man heard them speak in his own language. And they were all amazed and marvelled, saying one to another, Behold, are not all these which speak Galilaeans? And how hear we every man in our own tongue, wherein we were born ? we do hear them speak in our tongues the wonderful works of God. And they were all amazed, and were in doubt, saying one to another, What meaneth this? Others mocking said, These men are full of new wine. But Peter standing up with the eleven, lifted up his voice and said unto them." All the disciples engaged in communicating the wonderful works of God, then God raised up Peter to preach to the crowd on this occasion. This does not sanction the staging of preaching the gospel.

Personal evangelism was the daily practice of the apostles and disciples. Feet were made for walking, yes these members of the body were made for that purpose. They are to be used for walking to those in need. That is the only sure and safe way to bring good news to them. This is the method God would use to do good to His creation through His people. However there are those who would not agree; they would find fault with personal evangelism, charging that it is fishing for souls with a hook. Some would even claim that it does more harm than good. Would they withstand the apostle Paul to his face because he had shown and taught publicly and from house to house. Some would go to the limit and limit preaching of the gospel to that of staging meetings, and rule against personal evangelism. They would claim that the New Testament method of evangelism is that of the net. They equate the preaching of the gospel to a crowd of people, as casting out the gospel net to catch souls, to that of fishermen casting out a net to catch fish. They fish for one hour in the same place every Sunday evening hoping souls will come in to get caught. The rest of the week they make new nets. The fishing ceases. Does not nature teach that fishermen go to where the fish are to be found. Does not the Bible teach that the apostles, who fished for fish in boats, left the fishing for fish to go fishing for men they went two by two to preach the gospel of the kingdom of God to the lost tribes of Israel and later dragnetted the city of Jerusalem teaching and preaching Jesus Christ in the public place and from house too house. They went every day to where souls were to be found and preached the gospel to each and every creature.

Such had a right vision of God; a right mind toward God and the righteousness of God in doing that which is good and right to every creature. Whilst those that have a limited view of God doing that which is good and right to a limited few, those chosen to come into a relationship with God, those chosen to believe, those chosen to seek God, those chosen to come into a gospel meeting, they will limit their evangelism to staging the preaching of the gospel. They that would limit evangelism to staging the preaching of the gospel in halls, tents or the open-air, and would rule against personal evangelism, would be guilty of silencing the prophets see Amos 2:12-16, ver 12 and also 3:1-8 also 7:12,13 ands also Jer.11:21. In doing so they are not only stifling evangelism but also quenching the Spirit of God. Should the children of God obey them? God forbid. They must along with Peter say – "we ought to obey God rather than men." They will then go forth to preach the gospel to every creature; the poor, those humble enough to hear the truth and poor enough to accept it; to heal the broken-hearted, those whose love for life has been greatly shattered; to preach deliverance to the captives, those in bondage to sinful habits; recovery of sight to the blind, those that are in the dark as to their need; to set at liberty them that are in heaviness through different experiences, and preach the acceptable year of the Lord, that today is the day of salvation.

They will launch out into the deep and cast down their nets as directed by our Lord and drag the streets of their neighbourhood for souls in deep need. Just as the early disciples dragnetted the city of Jerusalem, so also the servants of God will preach the gospel to every creature. They will not limit fishing to one hour per week. Nor will they limit the Spirit of God doing right to the few connected to the children of God by the ties of nature. Nor will they limit the Spirit of God to ministering righteousness in one place. They will not stifle the operation of the Spirit. They will not wait for souls to come unto them that they might do them good and communicate the goodness of God. They will obey the Lord's commandment - "go into all the world and preach the gospel to every creature. He that believeth and is baptised shall be saved; but he that believeth not shall be damned" Mark 16:15,16. and also "Go ye therefore, and teach all nations, baptizing them in the name of the Father, and of the Son, and of the Holy Ghost: Teaching them to observe all things whatsoever I have commanded you: and, lo, I am with you alway, [even] unto the end of the world. Amen" Math 28:19,20. The apostles were obedient "And they departed from the presence of the council, rejoicing that they were counted worthy to suffer shame for his name. And daily in the temple, and in every house, they ceased not to teach and preach Jesus Christ." Acts 5:41,42. The apostle Paul did rightly state "how I kept back nothing that was profitable [unto you], but have shewed you, and have taught you publickly, and from house to house, testifying both to the Jews, and also to the Greeks, repentance toward God, and faith toward our Lord Jesus" Christ Acts 20:20,21

The Spirit of God had the apostle further declare "For there is no difference between the Jew and the Greek: for the same Lord over all is rich unto all that call upon him. For whosoever shall call upon the name of the Lord shall be saved. How then shall they call on him in whom they have not believed? and how shall they believe in him of whom they have not heard? and how shall they hear without a preacher? And how shall they preach, except they be sent? as it is written, How beautiful are the feet of them that preach the gospel of peace, and bring glad tidings of good things! But they have not all obeyed the gospel. For Esaias saith, Lord, who hath believed our report? So then faith [cometh] by hearing, and hearing by the word of God. But I say, Have they not heard? Yes verily, their sound went into all the earth, and their words unto the ends of the world. But I say, Did not Israel know? First Moses saith, I will provoke you to jealousy by [them that are] no people, [and] by a foolish nation I will anger you. But Esaias is very bold, and saith, I was found of them that sought me not; I was made manifest unto them that asked not after me." Rom.10:12- 20 also "For yourselves, brethren, know our entrance in unto you, that it was not in vain: But even after that we had suffered before, and were shamefully entreated, as ye know, at Philippi, we were bold in our God to speak unto you the gospel of God with much contention. For our exhortation [was] not of deceit, nor of uncleanness, nor in guile: But as we were allowed of God to be put in trust with the gospel, even so we speak; not as pleasing men, but God, which trieth our hearts. For neither at any time used we flattering words, as ye know, nor a cloke of covetousness; God [is] witness: Nor of men sought we glory, neither of you, nor [yet] of others, when we might have been burdensome, as the apostles of Christ. But we were gentle among you, even as a nurse cherisheth her children: So being affectionately desirous of you, we were willing to have imparted unto you, not the gospel of God only, but also our own souls, because ye were dear unto us. For ye remember, brethren, our labour and travail: for labouring night and day, because we would not be chargeable unto any of you, we preached unto you the gospel of God. Ye [are] witnesses, and God [also], how holily and justly and unblamably we behaved ourselves among you that believe: As ye know how we exhorted and comforted and charged every one of you, as a father [doth] his children, That ye would walk worthy of God, who hath called you unto his kingdom and glory. For this cause also thank we God without ceasing, because, when ye received the word of God which ye heard of us, ye received [it] not [as] the word of men, but as it is in truth, the word of God, which effectually worketh also in you that believe."1Thessalonians 2:1-13.

From the foregoing scriptures, it is clear that evangelism requires teaching and preaching. In other words showing and telling, and should be done personally.

**There is no scripture, no commission to go into all the world and preach the gospel to every creature that comes to hear it**. There is no directive for staging the righteousness of God. To do so is to deny the sovereignty of the Spirit of God.

In order to fulfil the commission to preach the gospel to every creature, the servant of God should set forth to preach the gospel to every creature that meets him in the public place and every one that he meets on going from house to house. He (the Holy Spirit) that letteth will open every meeting by letting it be brief or by extending it for His purpose, so that there is no need to manipulate or force an entrance. The messenger can readily discern from the free discourse that the meeting has been convened by God. He can then focus his attention on the one in need and deal with him personally. The apostle Paul did likewise, for he was gentle with each one just as a nurse cherisheth her children. He exhorted, comforted and charged every one of them, as a father doth with his children. He dealt with each one individually. He didn't deal with them en mass. That would be ineffective. He was affectionately desirous of each and every one. His brotherly love was personal. That required handling the word of life relative to each soul, so that each could hear and see with their own eyes, behold and comprehend. It required the servant of God giving of himself, his time, treasure and talents to go to each and every one in need whether he be Jew or Greek, for he served the same Lord who is rich unto all that call upon Him. It required the servant going to the one in need, to bring him glad tidings of good things.

He dealt with each and every one at the right time. That is God's time and is known only to God and is the perfect time to drop a word in season. Good news brought at any other time is only news. How beautiful are the feet of them preach the gospel of peace and bring glad tidings of good things to the one in need at the right time. That cannot be said of one that waits for those in need to come to him at his time. For such an one to come to hear a preacher, his feet would have to be beautiful. If he is lame or halt and helpless then he is without hope. Such an one lay by the pool of Bethseda. When the Lord Jesus Christ came and saw him and knew that he had been a long time in that state, saith unto him – "wilt thou be made whole?" That was a beautiful day for that man. To him the Lord's feet were beautiful for they brought hope to him who had no hope, and he rejoiced to tell that it was Jesus that made him whole.

When Peter and John went up together into the temple at the hour of prayer, they went to where the people were to be found. One lame from birth was brought there, not to hear the preachers, but to seek alms. God convened for him a meeting with two of His servants. They being in the way the Spirit lead them to meet that one at the right time, at the right place. That being the gate to the temple which is called beautiful. Truly that was a beautiful place for that poor cripple that day and to him the feet of Peter and John were beautiful for they brought him not silver and gold, but the word of God and to faith in Jesus Christ and he leaped up with joy, praising God.

Like the apostles and disciples, the people of God must obey the command to go to those in need. We are without excuse for we are well equipped; we are enriched by Him in everything, in all utterance and all knowledge and we are indwelt by the Holy Spirit. Under His guidance we will be lead to one in need. We do not need to minister to all in order to minister to that one. Most times the one in need is alone and needs to be there. For it is there God can speak to him without disturbance from those around. Remember that when God was preparing Moses and the Apostle Paul, He took each to the back side of the desert; yea back away from man as far as possible. We must go to where the one in need abides and there show him the way and help him to understand, just as Philip went to the Ethiopian eunuch and showed him the way and helped him to understand. Truly, it was beautiful feet that brought glad tidings of good things to that one from a far country.

Philip having consecrated himself to doing right was so sincere that he left his family and the comfort of his home, and crossed a desert on foot to meet this man that was unknown to him. He was so eager to do good and communicate to him that he ran. To do so Philip sacrificed much. For the child of God to have beautiful feet he or she must give of their time, talents and treasure - there must be sacrifice. Forgetting not that our Lord made the supreme sacrifice to do you and I the greatest good, and forgetting not that to do good and communicate is a sacrifice with which God is well pleased, then we would go forth to pass the time of our sojourn in the fear of displeasing God and learn of Him that did always those things that doth please the Father.

Our Lord sacrificed His time to be kind to all and went out of His way to do good to a Samaritan woman in the city of Sychar. He engaged her in conversation by asking of her the simplest of favours. In a similar way, we seeking to do a sinner the great favour of showing him his need of salvation and telling him about the goodness of God, can seek a personal favour by asking that one to take a tract; especially one you have written, and more especially if it is an abridged version of the message that God has given you. For if allowed of God to present the full message, it may be used as a back up to what you have already communicated and which the Holy Spirit may use to bring to remembrance in a time acceptable. It may be used of God to show the truth of salvation to a deaf person or one to whom you have not been allowed to communicate the gospel for reasons known only to God. The silent messenger must not take the place of the messenger. God has deigned to do good and communicate through His people and not through tracts. They were not used in the early Church to herald the glad tidings.

Admittedly the early Church did not have the facilities for printing. Nevertheless the gospel spread from Jerusalem to Judea and to the further end of the earth, without the use of tracts. It was most effectively spread by word of mouth then, and can be now. But the people of God have failed in their responsibilities, and will excuse themselves saying souls have been reached and saved by reading a tract. But then again souls have been reached and saved in missions conducted by unsaved preachers. Now we know that we should be made all things that we might by all means save some, but some means are not commendable. The servant of God when commended for handing out tracts is embarrassed, for he knows that this is not his ministry and that it is not as effective as some imagine.

The devil knows also, and being quick to copy God, he uses God's most effective way, and so he sends his ambassadors from door to door propagating his doctrines, but he does not use tracts. They don't provide explanations of misunderstood truths, but unfortunately they do provide the child of God with an excuse for shirking his responsibilities, and as a result of the failure of God's people in this Laodicean age, God has used tracts to make known His goodness to a world that is without knowledge of God. It is to the shame of the people of God.

Man's conscience enables him to reason what is right and what is not right. He knows that it is the will of God for his people to do good and communicate, and that the early Church taught and preached the gospel from house to house, and he reasons that is good and right, yet he fails to do so and that is sin. The Holy Spirit will convict him of his sin in not doing good. He salves his conscience with such excuses as '*I don't have that gift*' or '*I give out tracts*'. He will seek to justify his excuse by calling it a reason, asserting faith cometh by hearing the word of God, and tracts contain the word of God and that God can use the silent messenger to convict, convince, and convert sinners. He will go further by asserting that, this is how God in these last days, is going to reach the lost, who will not come into the gospel meeting. and that is his reason for giving out tracts. There is some truth in what he says, but it is not God's ordained way of preaching the gospel to every creature. God's way is set forth simply in His word – "how shall they hear without a preacher? and how shall they preach, except they be sent? as it is written, How beautiful are the feet of them that preach the gospel of peace, and bring glad tidings of good things."Rom.10:14-15. The silent messenger does not have beautiful feet, and cannot give reasonable answers to questions, nor say it in love, nor with the right mind, in the right manner, nor does God hold it responsible for doing so; nor does it contain the fundamental truths needed to equip one to make a wise choice, for most gospel tracts are testimonies of the saving grace of God. All are about the gospel, but none present the gospel. It cannot be said of them that "ye know the manner of their entrance in." see 1Thes.1:5 - 2:11. They that presume, that by giving out tracts, they are fulfilling the great commission and claim that they are fully persuaded in their own mind that this is their ministry, are vain in their imagining for they have fully deceived themselves into shirking their responsibilities.

Gospel tracts have a use. They can be used as a means of contact. They can be used as a means of making oneself available to help an enquirer (provided he has his address on it). They can be used to make known the location of the local assembly. The silent messenger should not be sent in the place of the servant. The Ethiopian eunuch had the word of God in his hand, more sufficient than any tract, yet God sent an evangelist to show him the way of salvation. Philip presented truth in an orderly fashion and then explained it so that the one in need could understand the will of God and choose to accept it. It is the duty of every child of God to do likewise and do good and communicate the righteousness of God. Each must be able to present his message simply and plainly for each and every one to understand. He should be willing and able to give an answer to every man that asketh a reason of the hope that is in him, with meekness and fear. He should do so in a manner that is well pleasing to the Lord.

# The Right Manner of Righteousness

Each and every day our Lord went forth, departed to a solitary place and prayed. Morning by morning God opened His ear and He was as the learned. One day He learned that He must needs go through Samaria to do good to a resident of Sychar. We Christians should follow our Lord. Each morning we should rise up, and pray with thanksgivings unto our God for guidance and preparation. Daily the child of God needs revival of the soul, renewal of the spirit, restrengthening of the inner man and reassurance of the Lord's presence with him. Otherwise he will be as Samson, who went forth as before not knowing that the Lord had left him.

Zeal and enthusiasm will not suffice to sustain the servant who goes forth in his own strength. At the first sign of trouble he will feint and flounder and flee back home just as the young John Mark. It stopped his service for a time. It could stop one's service for good. The flesh is weak and appeals to the praise of man, but that will not sustain him in the storm of scorn, sarcasm and shame. He needs to rely solely on the Lord to uphold him. He needs divine power not only to protect him, but to control and empower him and enable him to behave himself in a manner that is well pleasing to our Lord. He needs to be filled with the Spirit.

The Spirit filled servant will not rush off to serve, but will continue in the place of the Holy. There the Spirit of God will occupy his mind with the greatness and goodness of God, and will fill his heart with love, adoration and appreciation of God. Worship must precede service; this is a divine principle. There must be a going in to the Lord before going out with our Lord. There must be a revelling in the love of the Lord before a revealing of the love of the Lord. The young convert, who would turn the world up side down, would do well to learn this principle, and learn to worship God. "For God seeketh true worshippers, they that shall worship God in spirit and in truth." John 4:23. The word of God does not mention that God seeks servants, but it does state that God deigns to use such and desires that they be found faithful. They must walk worthy of their calling: they must walk worthy of being called Children of God. Their manner of doing right must be well pleasing to the God. It must be Christlike.

Our Lord being Holy, harmless and undefiled, He was without blemish and without spot. He was devoid of imperfection. He was transparent as the Jasper stone. He was open in all His dealings. Since God hath chosen that we us Christians should be holy and without blame before Him in love, we must be cleansed of all defilement that we might be open and transparent in our dealings with all souls.

Our Lord being righteous, loved righteousness and thirsted after righteousness and hide not righteousness within Him. He went about healing all manner of sickness and all manner of disease. We that have been made righteous and have righteousness imparted to us, should thirst after righteousness and seek to do good to each and every one and tell them of the goodness of our God. We must be willing to suffer for the cause of righteousness and be bold in our God to preach the gospel of God with much contention.

Our Lord being human (yet divine) wearied with the journey sat on a well. There cometh a woman of Samaria to draw water John 4:4-42. Even though He was tired, He tired not in well doing. It behoves us Christians to abound in doing good, and cease not to teach and preach Jesus Christ in the public place and from house to house.

Our Lord being just was no respecter of persons. He went about doing good to all. Unlike His own who had no dealings with Samaritans our Lord dealt with this woman. So also we servants of God should seek to do good to all, showing no preference for kindred, tongue, people, nation or creed. "All souls are mine" said the Lord (Ezek.18:4), and were created for God's pleasure, to come into relationship with God and live to please God throughout eternity. That is the birth right of every human being born into this world. Our mission is to minister in love the word of reconciliation to each and everyone.

Our Lord being all loving, loved all, even the most unlovable. He being affectionately desirous of helping this woman, sought to tell her of the gift of God. So also we brethren beloved of the Lord must love every one and be willing to give of our time, talents and treasure to do good to one and all at all times.

Our Lord being from above was above all in thought, word and deed. He was above saying anything that would offend. He was above being offended by this woman's comments. He talked with her at the well, in the open, not in the shade, nor in a corner, or behind closed doors. He was above suspicion. We whose conversation is in heaven must be above saying anything that would offend, and be above being offended. We must also be above doing anything that will cause suspicion.

Our Lord being meek, He was given to forbearance and gently made entrance into this woman's life by asking a simple favour of her. Likewise we that would do good, could seek gently to open a conversation by simply offering one a gospel tract.

Our Lord being gracious, He ceased not to do favours and He did so courteously and politely. All did bear Him witness and wondered at the gracious words which proceeded out of His mouth. It behoves us His brethren to do favours and deal graciously with all souls. The people will wonder at our manner of conversation and we shall find favour with them.

Our Lord being the faithful witness bore witness to the truth at all times. We that would be faithful witnesses to our Lord must bear witness to the truth at all times. Fearing displeasing our Lord, we speak not as pleasing men, nor using flattering words as we seek to persuade souls.

Our Lord being allwise He did not yield to talking about Himself nor seeking His own glory. Instead, He talked to the woman of the vanity of life and the hope of a better life. We ambassadors of Christ should wisely avoid talking about ourselves and concentrate on speaking forth the wonderful works of our Lord and God.

Our Lord being omniscient knows what is in man. He knows that all have sinned and He knows all the sins of each. He reminds her of a sinful past. We know not with whom we speak. But we do know that all have sinned and we would remind each that the Bible declares that "all have sinned" Rom.3:23, and show them the consequences of sin.

Our Lord being the Prince of Peace and having made peace with this woman maintained that peace throughout their discourse. He did not let Himself be drawn into discussing matters that would distress her and disrupt the meeting. Blessed are we ambassadors of Christ who try to make peace with all and maintain that peace. We avoid foolish questions and striving about the law and discussing affairs of this world, which engender disputings. We give no occasion to anger and annoy our subject. It has been said that *'fishermen don't cast stones in the water*. Instead we cast wholesome words for our subject to feed upon.

Our Lord being sovereign had all power to control this meeting without imposing His will upon this woman. He permitted her to express herself, yet restrained her from having free course. Then in a dignified and majestic manner He brought her back on the line of eternal blessing. Likewise we fishers of men should seek to take control of each meeting and keep our subject on line of hearing the good news of the goodness of God.

There was a dignity about our Lord's entrance upon that scene of time. It was not in vain, for it brought blessing to that woman and many. We that follow our Lord and fish for souls in the same manner, have this confidence that our entrance upon them will be effectual just as that of Paul and Silas.

Both these servants of the Lord redeemed from a vain manner of living, followed the Lord and sought to please God at all times. That was their practice and they preached what they practised. Their practice gave credence to their preaching. They preached the gospel in a manner that becomes the gospel of Christ, and the Thessalonian converts in every place followed their ensample, so that they needed not to speak anything. They needed not to speak of their ministry: no need to publish abroad their exploits. The Thessalonian Christians became not only followers of Paul and Silas, but also of the Lord and were ensamples to all believers in Macedonia, Achaia and in every place their faith toward God was spread abroad. For they themselves showed of what manner of entering in Paul and Silas had unto them. It was effectual and the apostle Paul under inspiration of the Holy Spirit beseeches the people of God saying "be ye followers of me even as I also of Christ."

Like begets like, to this nature bears witness. The character of the worker is imprinted in his work. The cobbler that is careless will care little about what others think of his workmanship. Whereas the true master craftsman that seeks the mastery of his craft, is careful and pays particular attention to every detail and wants to produce a fine finished work. His workmanship is readily recognized. The apprentice will seek to follow his master. So, it is in the spiritual realm. The worker that follows the Lord will manifest in a measure the moral glories of his Lord, and in turn it will be reproduced and reflected in his work. Just as Paul's manner of living left its imprint in his workmanship.

The right manner of doing right was not in vain, for it was an ensample to the new converts, and it not only abode for the time of their sojourn there in the flesh, but it will abide for ever. The servant of God who does right by the right means, for the right motive in the right manner will build into the church that which will abide forever. Those converted through the ministry of the Holy Spirit working through and in harmony with them will beget converts characterized by a right manner, with the right motive and doing right by the right means.

Those that preach a soft insincere conviction lacking gospel will beget insincere double-minded followers more like the preacher. Those that preach a hard judgment gospel will beget hardhearted preachers that will reproduce their work. One such preacher on seeing a young man approach, greeted him saying - *'young man, I tell you are going to hell'*, and when preaching from the platform, he would draw aside an imaginary curtain and ask the unsaved to look into hell. That young man accepted the hard gospel and in turn preached a hard gospel using the same gimmickry.

The servants of God should not be foolish and follow such preachers, but follow our Lord and walk circumspectly not as fools, but wise as serpents, yet harmless as doves. We should teach and preach on the outside of the door, and politely refuse all invitations to go inside, thus safe guarding our testimony. We must teach and preach on the door step, irrespective of whether the weather be favourable or not, for the meeting may be convened by God. Remember "he that observeth the wind shall not sow; and he that regardeth the clouds shall not reap. As thou knowest not what the way of the spirit, how the bones in the womb of her who is with child, even so thou knowest not the works of God, who maketh all." (see Ecc.11:4). God works with people on wet days as well as dry days.

Some do err and unwisely teach and preach in the house. They go where angels fear to tread, and foolishly go where sinners might entice one, and a strange woman might flatter with her words. Remember her house might incline unto death, and her paths unto the dead. "None that go unto her may return again."Prov.2:18,19. This death does not mean break in relationship with God but it means break of fellowship with God, to exist as one without a relationship with God; dead to the blessings that come from God, and the privileges that God would give one. No further the privilege of serving God. The child of God must realize, that just as the people of this world were wolves when our Lord sent forth the disciples to preach the gospel of the kingdom of heaven to the lost sheep of Israel, so also He sends His people forth in the midst of wolves to preach the gospel of the glories of Christ to every creature. They should also accept His exhortation to be wise as serpents, and harmless as doves. They should learn of our Lord, and those that followed Him such as the apostle Paul, and also of one who typified the Lord, namely Joseph.

When his master's wife cast her eyes upon Joseph and said – "lie with me". Joseph refused, for he knew that it was sin against God and of great wickedness to lie with her, but he also knew not to be with her. Nevertheless, she persisted, and when she knew that she had Joseph alone in a chamber of the house, she reached out in lust to take hold of him, but he fled and she only got hold of a piece of his garment. Yet it was sufficient for her in the gall of bitterness to use in falsely accusing him. A frightening thought that should move one to be wise, and be filled with the Spirit.

He that makes the mistake of not taking the time to prepare, and goes forth not knowing that the Lord had left him, is vulnerable to temptation and sin. Joseph didn't, because the Lord was with him. When tempted, the Spirit of God will provide a way of escape, and if the servant does not seize it, then the pleasures of sin will seize him. As the light goes out to do such evil deed, one's light will go out in the neighbourhood. Bad news travels faster than sound, and the darkness of ones testimony will fall beyond his neighbourhood. His service will come to an abrupt end. To move to another part of the vineyard will not help, for the Lord will no longer put that one in trust with the gospel, unless he repents. Then again, ye know that Esau, who for gratification of the flesh sold his birthright, and "ye know how that afterward, when he would have inherited the blessing, he was rejected: for he found no place of repentance, though he sought it carefully with tears."Heb.12:17.

When a child of God falls into sin, he falls out of fellowship with the Lord God, and with the people of God, and slides back in knowing, trusting and loving his Lord. Such a backsliden state is worse than the first, for the unsaved know not what is right, but the child of God knows what is right, but can't do it, and of all people he is most cursed. He has lost his right to the privileges and responsibilities of the Father; he has lost also his right of the Godly line through whom blessing should flow to the world; he has also lost his right to represent the saints to God, his priesthood; he has lost his right to do right and please God. Furthermore, if one rejects the tempting of an evil and adulteress woman, she can take vengeance with a despiteful heart and eject one into the world with false accusations. The world that knows him not, because it knew not the Lord, will believe the woman, and gather one up and cast his testimony into the fire of man's wrath.

Now the wisdom of our Lord was manifest in sending out the disciples, two by two, exhorting them to be wise as serpents. One needs to be as wise as the old serpent the devil himself for it is who will be seeking to seduce one, and put out ones light and stop his service, and in turn stop God doing right through that child of God. He should also be wise enough not to stoop to using flattering words or guile to woo and win the unrighteousness. The apostle Paul even though he was affectionately desirous of all, did not stoop to flattery, nor did he covet any for his own advancement and seek by subtle and sly means to win them to himself. But having renounced the hidden things of dishonesty, not walking in craftiness, nor handling the word of God deceitfully, but by manifestation of the truth commended himself to every man's conscience in the sight of God. But though rude in speech, yet not in knowledge he and his coworkers were thoroughly made manifest among those to whom they preached the gospel. 2Cor.11: 6. So must we be open in all our dealings and deal with all in the open and faithfully bear witness to the truth.

Being filled with the Spirit of power and of love and of a sound mind, we in love for our Lord obey His command to go into the world and preach the gospel, and in love for man we preach to every one as allowed of God. With power and a sound mind we preach Jesus Christ, warning every man, teaching every man in all wisdom; that we may present every man perfect in Christ Jesus. Just as our Lord loved the leper and put forth his hand and touched the untouchable, so we should want to love the lepers of society, those filthy in thought, word and deed and even though it vexes our souls to listen to their vile language and know of their depraved conduct, we must reach out to woo and win all sinners and touch their heart so that they'll want to be cleansed of their sin and their loathesome manner of living. This does not mean going purposely amongst them. There is no special ministry to those caught up in sex, booze, drugs, the occult, and the cults. Such ministries are man-made. They have mushroomed in modern times; unheard of in the early Church when booze and drugs were available. Such ministries are a crumb of comfort from the devil to deceive the child of God into thinking he is doing the will of God, whilst all the time he is wasting valuable God given time. Instead of being in the way that the Spirit may lead him, such ministries are in the way of the child of God being lead by the Spirit to the one he must need meet that day.

Just as love moved our Lord to cross the troubled sea to tame the untamable and restore one mentally deranged to his right mind, so must we cross seas of trouble and suffer the slings and arrows of outrageous fortune and suffer barrages of abuse, and with the patience of Job and power from on high tenderly tackle the problem and seek to teach those bewitched bothered and bewildered, of peace through Jesus Christ - He is Lord of all. We should not be shy, as one ashamed, but as Spirit filled servants stand up for our Lord, for what is right, and what is the truth. We have nothing of which to be ashamed except our sinful past.

We should not be ashamed of the gospel, "for it is the power of God unto salvation to everyone that believeth" Rom.1:16. It is the righteousness of God. We should not be ashamed of the testimony of our Lord, for all that He said and did was above reproof, and only He could say – "which of you convinceth me of sin?" John 8:46. It will serve us well to remember this, for there will come a time when some one will pour out their wrath, scorn and shame on us for daring to draw nigh unto them and disturb and drag them away from what they are doing, to hear about that which they deem foolishness. Cast down but not destroyed, yet rather than take up arms against a sea of trouble, we should politely take our leave. It is then that the enemy would have us quit and head for home. But it is then the Spirit of Christ upholds and comforts us by reminding us that we have nothing of which to be ashamed, and lifts us above our circumstances and above retaliating and comforts us by encouraging us to forgive them, for they know not what they do. It is then we comfort ourselves in the Lord when we remember that there was no one more despised and rejected of men than our Lord and there was no time in which one suffered more than when our Lord uttered these words. Remembering that Paul suffered being shamefully treated at Philippi, "yet being bold in our God he spoke the gospel with much contention." 1Thes.2:2. So revived and with renewed strength, we regain our composure and with steadfastness of heart and soundness of mind, claim the victory through our Lord Jesus Christ, and remembering that we are debtor both to the wise and the unwise, we head straight for the next door.

He that will preach the gospel will do so with much contention. He will have to contend with the devil. One cannot expect to bear witness unto our Lord and the truth, and the god of this world cast a blind eye to it. "all that will live Godly in Christ Jesus shall suffer persecution." 2Tim.3:12. The door to door evangelist knows this truth from the word of God, but also from hard experience. But he also knows from the word of God and from experience, that the Lord delivers him out of them all. Our Lord also knows them that are His; they that are suffering for the cause of righteousness. The brethren may not know, for they that know their God never parade their exploits. They seek not to be known openly, and so one will not hear prayer being made for them in the public place.

One brother having ministered the word of God to the saints, exalting the love of the Lord, exposing the subtlety of the devil, within three days a man had him by the throat with the sentence of death upon him. Only the Lord and himself knew that the devil meant it for evil. But the Lord meant it for good, for He delivered him by bringing another on the scene at the perfect time - the right moment. Our Lord meant to use the experience for good, to perfect that soldier of the cross through sufferings, just as the captain of our salvation was made perfect through sufferings. That brother knows that salvation is a great salvation that goes far beyond saving him from eternal punishment, and saves him from the power of sin and the power of satan, for which cause he does not neglect so great salvation. Accordingly he gives more earnest heed to the things written for our learning, lest he should let slip and slip. He does not let slip any of God's promises, but relies solely on the Lord fulfilling each and every promise. Nor does he neglect to tell others of this great salvation, so the gospel that he preaches, whether in the public place or on the door step goes far beyond that of salvation from suffering in hell and the lake of fire, to major in salvation from sinning against God and doing evil, and from suffering the evil that the devil and the powers of evil would do man.

Gladly he knocks doors thirsting to do some one the greatest good by telling that one how he or she can come into relationship with God and be saved to the uttermost. He may knock two or three times. When there is no response he will place his tract where the occupant can find it. On the other hand when one appears, he may offer his tract while introducing himself, and saying, I'm giving out tracts and seeking to show people the need of salvation. This enables him to follow with the question – *'can you see the need for one to get saved?'* This is bound to cause a reaction or response, hopefully the latter. Those that react will do so depending on their disposition see ch.9C and should be dealt with accordingly.

Those who respond by accepting the tract and answering honestly – 'no I don't', the servant of God will set out to present his message. If he chooses to use the right message of righteousness as set forth in ch.5, then he will start by showing them that they were born separated from God and that they live to please themselves and the terrible consequences of doing so. Having told them the bad news, he will proceed to tell them the good news, concluding with an appeal to their will to accept the truth he has heard.

From the moment he introduces himself, by asking the simplest of favours, he unobtrusively takes control of the meeting. The Holy Spirit will enable him to do so, for it is He that is going to control the meeting. It is He who convened the meeting for the blessing of that poor soul. His subject not knowing the gift of God or the person with whom he is speaking will be apprehensive and will question the messenger. The servant will try to allay his fears and set him at ease by telling him that if he only knew the good that God wants to do him and that the one to whom he speaks is a servant of God, then he would gladly want to hear about it. His subject on further doubting the messenger may retort *'you are not able for such matters, Are you more able than my minister who supplies all my spiritual needs?'* The servant should be careful in how he answers such questions. When the woman at the well questioned our

Lord, saying – "art thou greater than our father Jacob, which gave us this well, and drank thereof himself." John 4:12 He could quite easily have shown her that He was greater than Jacob who had power with God and men, but He also had all authority in heaven and earth. Instead of being sidetracked into talking about Himself, He refrained from answering her question, but kept her on the track of blessing, by enlightening her to the fact that her way of life didn't satisfy. Then He immediately told her of a better way that will satisfy all her needs.

The servant of God must not be tempted into talking about himself, but instead respond by enlightening his subject to the truth that his present way of living is all vanity. Then he must wet his appetite by intimating to him of the way that will satisfy his every need. This should beget in him desire to hear more, just as it did with the woman. At that point the servant of God has got to the heart. He must get there and set it right before he grapples with the problem and presents the solution. Before his subject hears the good news, he must need hear the bad news.

Our Lord, having got to the heart of the woman, reminds her of her past, then draws to her attention that she is living in sin. At that moment, she was convicted, her conscience pricked, and just as a fish when pricked with the hook, darts off up stream to escape, so the woman darted off into religion for refuge. Acknowledging that he was a prophet, and seeking to justify her position saying our fathers worshipped in this mountain and seeking to question His position said – "ye say, that in Jerusalem is the place where men ought to worship." John 4:20. Our Lord did not contradict her, and did not make any apologies for where His own worshipped. He did not follow her; He did not engage in religious discussion, but straightway brought her back on the line of blessing by telling her that God is not worshipped in buildings. He is worshipped in spirit and in truth. She suspecting this will happen in a time yet future said I know that when Messiah cometh He will teach us all things. Then He revealed to her that the time is now, for He is Messiah. Oh the exceeding riches of His grace in His kindness to such an one in need, and oh the excellency of His majesty in controlling this meeting.

We who in times past were as others know not the past details of one's life, but we do know that our subject was born a sinner, has a sinful past and is presently living in sin. We cannot convict him or raise an anxious thought, so we parade the wrong doings of Rom.1:29-31., before his mind's eye and leave it to the Holy Spirit to convict him of his sin. The moment that his conscience is pricked, he will fight hard against it and fearing further reproof he will dart off screaming out justifications saying – '*my people are members of that church up there.*' Then he will attack the messenger saying – '*you think your church is the right one.*' He is trying to direct the servant's attention away from himself. He is trying to get off the hook. We fishers of men avoid foolish questions and strivings about the law. We don't want to loose our trend of thinking, lest we loose him. We allow him to express himself, yet not allow him free course. Otherwise he will lead us into a weed bed of religious confusion, where he can find refuge from the truth.

Keeping him on a taut line and with the gracious help of the Holy Spirit, we sense the time is right to draw him slowly back to where we want him, back unto our own line of thinking. - the way of blessing. We tell him that nobody and no body of people can save him, but there is hope in God "who will have all men to be saved and to come unto the knowledge of the truth."1Tim.2:4. We further comfort him with the great truth that God is "not willing that any should perish, but that all should come to repentance."2Pet.3:9. Then we proceed to show him the goodness of God that will hopefully lead him to repentance.

Now, whilst there is life in the fish, it can take off again. The fisherman will try again to get control of it and draw it back and into the net. Many fish are lost in the netting. It must be brought to the net and not the net to the fish and he must not be brought too soon.

Whilst there is life still left in the flesh, and if further truth pricks our subject and he takes off, we fishers of men resume working with him until he is spent, yea at his tethers end, at the end of wanting to live to please himself. When he comes to that place of repentance then we seek to net him with the challenge to his will. Does he want to live to please God ? The man that sincerely wants to please God, is ready to be netted and to be translated into the kingdom of the Son of God

When the fish is landed, it is kept in a net, then transferred into a place especially prepared for it's conservation. It is a trophy to be cherished. The fisherman must ensure that the fish has every thing it needs for its well being. There must be an adequate and continuous supply of food, both when young and adult. The fish also needs cover into which it can dive when danger threatens. It also requires facilities for reproducing. But before it starts reproducing, there must be no manhandling of the fish, it must be treated very carefully and delicately and tenderly, otherwise it loses scales and weakens. It also needs protection from disturbance. When they start to reproduce, they can be man handled, yet with care, for they are still very sensitive.

So it is when we fishers of men land a trophy of grace, we keep close watch over it until he can be transferred into a place specially prepared for his conservation. That place is the local assembly of the people of God, prepared by God. It is the place where he can conserve all his energies to fulfilling his purpose of being created, living to please God. It is there, we can ensure that he has everything he needs for his well-being. There he will receive adequate and continuous supply of food (the truth), for it is the ground and pillar of truth, it is there he will be fed the truth until he can feed for himself. There will be no withholding the truth of gathering unto the Lord in assembly pattern, and how one must behave in the house of God. Nor will he be held back from expressing his true love for the Lord Jesus Christ. Nor will the truth be mingled with untruth and the vain imaginings of man. He will not be told to say one thing and think another. Such only weaken his stance for righteousness and he will not be able to woo the unrighteous and win them to righteousness. He will not be able to reproduce. He needs cover into which he can dive, when dangerous teaching from without threatens his very purpose of living to do that which is good and right and please God. He requires facilities to reproduce. Within every child of God there is that desire to see other sons brought to glory. This desire must be fostered, it must be fed and given full expression. He must be encouraged and exhorted to discern the gift that he has been given by the Holy Spirit, and challenged to use it, just as Paul exhorted, encouraged and challenged Timothy to stir up the gift that is within him.

The work of winning souls is the work of faith in the Holy Spirit convening a meeting between a servant of God and an heir of salvation regarding faith in Jesus Christ. There is no reasoning required on the part of the servant of God. No sales psychology - the more presentations the more professions. Nothing is left to the ingenuity of man. No need for man to arrange a meeting. No need for him to enquire where his subject lives. No need to follow him up. It is the work of the Lord from start to finish.

Each day we that would follow our Lord go forth intent on communicating the goodness of God to every creature. We go to where souls are to be found, that is the public place or from house to house. We need to seek and find those that Spirit of God has sanctified to hear the truth. We may speak to many souls and be allowed of God to preach the gospel to 1 or 2 or more. These meetings are convened by God regarding faith in Christ and each lasts as long as the Spirit wills, so we fishermen can be wearied at the end of the day's fishing and will welcome the opportunity to come aside and rest awhile. It is then with prayer and supplications and thanksgivings we intercede on behalf of those whom we met in the way. It is then that the Spirit of our Lord will bring to remembrance each conversation. He will convince us of our mistakes, and seek to correct and instruct us in the right way that we might be perfect and thoroughly furnished unto further good works. This time alone with our Lord is precious to us, for not only do we use it to prepare to tackle future conquests, but also to study the word of God and to prepare to worship our God.

Fishing for men is a lifetime occupation that none ever master yet everyone should seek the mastery of it. This must not deter young or old converts who would see the need to do it and want to do it. One does not need to know all about fishing nor have the best of tackle in order to fish. One can start with little knowledge and a little line. The writer started with the simple line –"*all have sinned: ye are separated from God: and Christ Jesus hath once suffered for sins to bring you unto God.*" These are the three truths that God used to bring him into relationship with Himself. Immediately he started over against his own house to share these truths, and has been doing so ever since that day. He has sought to learn how to evangelise, to understand people, how to deal with them, how to present the gospel in a simple way that even the simplest can understand. In other words, how he can do that which is good and right, the right way. This is the greatest good. This should be the quest of each and every child of God. One's lack of knowledge of the scriptures or his lack of ability to deal with people should not deter him. Our Lord promises – "follow thou me and I will make you fishers of men."Math.4:19. We know that He is faithful that promised. Art thou? Are you following the Lord? 'are you fishing for men?'

It is the greatest work available to the sons of God. There is no other work like it. It is the Lord's work. It is the Lord working in and through His people. There is no greater challenge offered to the child of God than to do the greatest good. There is no work more rewarding than fishing for men. Each day as one heads for home he walks tall, yea above this world in the heavenlies full of joy and glory, for he has been doing something worthwhile for his Lord. When he sits down to mend his tackle, he recalls the things that happened that day and then realizes that here he is a simple mortal, being used by the Great God of Eternity, to effect change in the life of some poor soul; a change for good; a change that will last throughout eternity - No greater responsibility than to be entrusted by the Lord God. No greater sight than to see the Holy Spirit changing a human being before one's very eyes. To read of the Sovereignty of God is a joy but to see and know and experience it is a joy unspeakable. "The wind bloweth where it willeth, and thou hearest the sound of it, but canst not tell from where it cometh, so is every one that is born of the Spirit." John 3:8. He can see the effect of the Holy Spirit working in the lives of humans. He can see hard hearted herods being humbled to hear and hearken to the word of God and their hearts softly opened to accept the Lord Jesus Christ.

When shall these things be? When one does right the right way at the right time!

# The Right Moment of Righteousness

God is good and doeth good. He deigns to use His people to do good to all His creation. Being omniscient He knows all. He knows what is in man. He knows the state of each and every soul. He knows when one is in need and He knows who will accept His goodness. He knows where and when to do good. He knows the one to send. He knows not to send one that is insincere and untrustworthy. For the one in need can read such and will not accept their counsel. God will send one He can trust; one that is true and honest; one who is upright and will stand up for the truth. One who is prepared of the gospel of peace and prepared to climb mountains to bring glad tidings to one in need. Such a sincere and determined messenger is known and read of all, and his manner of living will give credence to his message and his counsel is worthy of all acceptation. To them that believe him, his feet will be beautiful. "How beautiful are the feet of them that preach the gospel of peace, and bring glad tidings of good things" Rom.10:15. There is a right time to bring good tidings, and that is when the one in need knows it, and wants help to meet that need. Any other time relegates the good tidings to mere tidings. Of a truth the writer of the book of Ecclesiastes did record –"To every thing a season, and a time to every purpose under the heaven?" Ecc.3:1. That same one, to whom God had given great wisdom and understanding said – "I have seen the travail, which God hath given to the sons of men to be exercised in it. He hath made every thing beautiful in His time." Ecc.3:10.

God created every thing and for His pleasure they are and were created. Every thing has a season in which its beauty is full. From its inception its beauty grows until it maximizes and then it begins to decline, and even though a thing of beauty is a joy, it is not for ever, for the beauty of each thing wanes with the passing of time. Since all beauty is for the glory of God, then God perpetuates beauty so that it is a joy forever. So each and every thing is brought to fruition in differing and succeeding times. Accordingly there is a time for the entrance of each creature into this world. Subsequently there is a time for each to depart from it. God has appointed man's bounds.

All humans are born into this world, to be vessels of mercy or wrath. God according to His foreknowledge will make the former into vessels of honour. He will change that soul to make it a thing of beauty that will for ever show forth the beauties of the Lord Jesus Christ. Since it was born of corruptible seed, it can only show forth the beauties of God for a season. Now all flesh is like grass, and all the glory of man like the flower of grass that flourishes for a season. Since it brings no lasting glory to God, then it must be born again of incorruptible seed, by the word of God, which liveth and abideth forever. God will prepare the heart of that soul to receive the word, and as people differ so also the preparation of their hearts. Known only to God is the work that goes into preparing each heart, and only God foreknows the heart that can be made good to receive sincerely the word and understand it and be made whole and bear fruit. The vast majority will not be made whole; they will not come that they might have life.

There is a time for the entrance of the word of truth into the heart of the soul and this is known only unto God. Preachers imagine that it is every time they preach and would use all kinds of tricks (stratagems) to make it happen. They are quick to quote today is the day of salvation and challenge their audience to decide today - 'I will' or 'I will not'. This is button-holing the unsaved into making a decision at a time not ordained by God, but by man. No preacher; no human being has authority from God to take such a liberty. This is an evil ploy used by preachers to coerce one into making a profession. But it is all vanity for a profession without repentance is false, to be manifest in due time.

There is a time to plant the seed of truth, and a time to water that sown: this is known only unto God, and it is He who will give the increase, in order that soul may grow in the knowledge of the truth,

There is a time to pluck that which has grown and bore fruit and ripened unto harvest.

There is a time to put an end to untruth.

There is a time to heal the broken-hearted, a heart that has been crushed to the point that it has almost lost the desire to live and love for the truth.

There is a time to break down self will that wants to do as it pleases and resist the truth.

There is a time to weep at souls bruised by untruth.

There is a time to laugh when truth triumphs over untruth.

There is a time to mourn over one who will not receive the truth, one who receives the grace of God in vain.

There is a time to dance with all one's might, when a soul accepts the truth and He who is the Truth, and is made wise unto salvation.

There is a time to cast away words of untruth.

There is a time to gather together words that are true.

There is a time to embrace those that will embrace the truth.

There is a time to refrain from embracing those that will embrace untruth and evil.

There is a time to get the truth of the matter, so that one can make a right judgment.

There is a time to lose all and to suffer loss of all things for the truth

There is a time to keep and hold fast that which is proven to be truth. There is a time to cast away every weight and the sin (of not accepting truth) that doth so easily beset us.

There is a time to rend an unprofitable alliance that is not based on the truth.

There is a time to sew the broken pieces of truth and strengthen the things that remain.

There is a time to keep silent, when you have nothing truthful to say.

There is a time to speak, when you have something truthful and right to say.

There is a time to love the truth and righteousness and the righteous.

There is a time to hate untruth and iniquity.

There is a time of war when the forces of evil will battle against the truth and what is good and right.

There is a time of peace when righteousness will triumph over unrighteousness; when righteousness rules in the heart.

"Blessed are they which do hunger and thirst after righteousness: for they shall be filled. Blessed are they which are persecuted for righteousness sake: for theirs is the kingdom of heaven Rejoice, and be exceeding glad: for great your reward in heaven." Matthew 5

With such comforting assurance, we can gladly accept Preacher's injunction – "cast thy bread upon the waters: for thou shalt find it after many days. Give a portion to seven, and also to eight; for thou knowest not what evil shall be upon the earth. If the clouds be full of rain, they empty upon the earth: and if the tree fall toward the south, or toward the north, in the place where the tree falleth, there it shall be. He that observeth the wind shall not sow; and he that regardeth the clouds shall not reap. As thou knowest not what the way of the spirit, how the bones in the womb of her that is with child: even so thou knowest not the works of God who maketh all. In the morning sow thy seed, and in the evening withhold not thine hand: for thou knowest not whether shall prosper, either this or that or whether they both alike good." Ecc.11:1-6.

Likewise Paul charged young Timothy saying – "I charge, therefore, before God, and the Lord Jesus Christ, who shall judge the quick and the dead at His appearing and His kingdom: preach the word; be instant in season, out off season; reprove, rebuke, exhort with long-suffering and doctrine." 2Tim.4:1,2. We must accept this same charge "for we are His workmanship, created in Christ Jesus unto good works, which God hath before ordained that we should walk in them." Eph.2:10.

Truly God is good and doeth good to all. Having done good to each child of God, He deigns to use each to do good to those outside the household of faith. God being all-loving, all knowing, all wise, all mighty and righteous knows when and where to do good. He knows the one that is in need and is willing to receive the goodness of God. He will set him aside unto belief of the truth. Just as He prepares a sinner He will also prepare a servant to do good to that soul. The Holy Spirit will convene a meeting for an acceptable time with both prepared.

The child of God should not arrange meetings, for he knows not what shall be on the morrow. Neither does he know the person, the need, the place nor the right time to deal with a soul. To do so is to stage good works. It is all vanity. For to do so would limit the Holy Spirit doing good to who, where, and when it pleases man. Likewise he should not determine before hand without being exercised by the Spirit to visit a home in order to face another with the need of salvation. Such a meeting even with the best intentions is all vanity, if the Spirit of God did not convene it. There should be no setting a definite day or time of the day for the preaching of the gospel. There should be no setting a definite place for the preaching of the gospel; no need to designate the church hall or the street corner for sinners to hear the word of God. There should be no selecting a definite brother to preach. There should be no setting the stage for the preaching of the gospel. There should be no staging the righteousness of God.

Man would like to gather a crowd of people into one place and preach to them, figuring that the more that hear the more will know. This is the thinking of salesmen who express it thus - the more one tells the more one sells. They that do so know not the way of the Spirit. But they do know that this is one way if not the best way to sell oneself and make a name.

Our Lord did not seek to make a name for Himself; but seeking to glorify the Father, and being all-knowing, He knew aforetime that He must needs go through Samaria there to meet a woman in need. He knew that the woman had walked according to the course of this world in the lusts of the flesh, fulfilling the desires of the flesh and mind. This woman in her thirst for love, life and happiness had tasted of the water from the well of man made marriage, and thirsted again. The fact that she had gone to that well 5 times and it was not well with her soul, she tried another time, proved the insufficiency of her way to satisfy her need. Truly she had tried the broken cisterns but oh how the waters failed. To lose one she loved, could have caused her to question – '*why God why?*' but to have it happen five times would have broken her heart and caused her to lose any faith she had in God. With a heart far from God she was without hope in this world and possibly without a friend. Not without guilt for she came to the well to draw water at noon, the right time to avoid drawing reproof and ridicule from the other women.

Our Lord knew the right time for her to be there and He also knew the right time to deal with her and to do her good. He knowing the right way to approach her began by asking of her the simplest of favours – "give me to drink." John 4:7. She unwilling to do Him any favor, or have any dealing with Him, in the gall of bitterness asked him saying – "How is it that thou, being a Jew, askest drink of me, which am a woman of Samaria? for the Jews have no dealings with the Samaritans." John 4:9.

Our Lord in loving kindness graciously answered her – "If thou knewest the gift of God, and who it is that saith to thee, Give me to drink; thou wouldest have asked of him, and he would have given thee living water." John 4:10. A word fitly spoken oh how good it is. It strangely warmed her enough to move her to want to do him the favor asked and also to induce her into wanting to converse, whilst she pondered on this living water. Knowing He had got her to the point of wanting to hear and talk, He then told her a fact of life that "whosoever drinketh of this water shall thirst again" John 4:13. and then compared it to a wonderful possibility saying – "whosoever drinketh of the water that I shall give him shall never thirst; but the water that I shall give him shall be in him a well of water springing up into everlasting life." John 4:14. This blessed prospect begot in her a want, she expressed – "Sir, give me this water, that I thirst not, neither come hither to draw."

Truly our Lord had brought her to the place where she not only wanted to hear but also wanted to have the gift that he could give her. This is the right place to be in order to receive the good that God would do. This is the right time to do that which is good and right. This is **the right moment of righteousness**. At that moment the heart has been prepared to hear and accept the good news. But in order that the good news be not robbed of its worth then one must be brought to realize the vanity of their way of life and their own worthlessness. Our Lord then told her - "Go, call thy husband." John 4:16 The woman did well in telling the truth saying "I have no husband." John 4:17 Our Lord then said "thou hast had five husbands; and he whom thou now hast is not thy husband." John 4:18. On reminding her of past thirsting and her present sinful state she was brought to realise that her manner of life did not satisfy and her conscience was pricked and she was convicted of her sin. Just as a fish when pricked with the hook darts off up stream to escape, she darted off up into the realm of religion to escape further reproof. Perceiving that he was more than mere man yea a man of God, she tried to console herself by claiming a form of godliness even though it differed from His.

Our Lord maintained control of the situation, permitted her to express herself, then most graciously brought her back on the line of his intent showing her the goodness of God. He used her comments to enlighten her to the fact that the place of worship is not important, and to tell her she knew not what she worshipped but the Jews do for they have the word of God, the words of life, the way of salvation. Then He revealed to her that God seeks true worshippers they that will worship God in spirit and in truth. The woman even though she knew not who or what she worshipped, told Him that she knew that Messiah is coming and He will tell her all things. When our Lord told her "I that speak unto thee am" John 4:26, she knew then that she had met Messiah, for He told her all things that ever she did. She believed Him.

With her mind staid on Him, she left her waterpot and with joy in her soul she calmly went forth to confess Him before men and witness unto the Lord in Samaria and live godly in this world. Truly this woman had met one greater than Jacob, the one who not only had power to change him but to change her and heal her broken heart and give her something to live for. To her the feet of Christ were beautiful, for they brought her glad tidings of good things and brought her everlasting life never to thirst again.

The servant of God knows not whom he must needs meet on any given day but the Holy Spirit knows, and He also knows where that person will be at a certain time. That servant must needs be like Philip, who being in the way the Spirit lead him to the right place at the right time when he beheld a man of Ethiopia, an eunuch of great authority under queen Candace was returning from worshipping in Jerusalem. The Holy Spirit knew the right place to send Philip, to the chariot in which the eunuch rode, and He knew the right moment to prompt his servant to move near to join this chariot; when he was being exercised in spiritual matters, reading the prophecy of Esaias. Now, the servant of God didn't know who was interested in such matters, nor did he know where he was to be found, but he knew that the person, the place, and the time are known only unto God. When prompted by the Holy Spirit he obeyed and moved close to the chariot.

Only God knows what would have happened if Philip had approached the Ethiopian sooner or later. This we know, the Ethiopian was made to understand the word of God and he gladly received what he understood. So he heard the good word at the good and acceptable time and that is the right time, yea the right moment to hear. He accepted the word of God and the Lord who is the Word and went on his way rejoicing at being brought the glad tidings of good things and being brought to faith in the Son of God, and to serve one greater than queen Candace. Truly the feet of Philip were beautiful to that Ethiopian Eunuch.

When Peter and John went up together into the temple, they entered by the gate called Beautiful and did meet one lame lying on the ground. Truly this man had been laid low physically, mentally and spiritually. for he had been brought low to beg, humble enough to listen to another and poor enough to receive counsel. This is the right place for blessing. When Peter and John entered into the life of this man they immediately fastened their interest on him and seeking his attention exhorted him saying '*look at us*'. This he did, and saw that these men were sincere; and that their exhortation was not of deceit, nor in guile, nor uncleanness. They spoke not as pleasing him; they did not use flattery, but were straight and honest. They were gentle and being affectionately desirous of him they would have imparted unto him of themselves such as they had they would have given him. The poor cripple saw that they were men of integrity and he took heed unto them, and at the right moment took them at their word and took them by the right hand and rose and walked.

That gate was rightly called beautiful and it was the right place for him to be that day, for it opened up a beautiful entrance into his life of two ambassadors for Christ. Their entrance was not in vain, for their manner moved him to want to hear and opened up a beautiful entrance for the word of God into his heart at the right moment. To this man the feet of Peter and John were beautiful for they brought him not silver and gold but to faith in the Lord God, and he who could in no wise stand upright, jumping up stood, walked and entered with them into the temple, walking and leaping and praising God.

In order for our Lord to continue doing good to His creation He deigns to use His people and seeks their cooperation. Each child of God should realize that it is not only their responsibility but a privilege to work together with the Lord God, the creator of heaven and earth and all that is therein. None should dare receive that grace in vain, that the ministry of righteousness be blamed. "No man, having put his hand to the plough and looking back, is fit for the kingdom of God." Lk.9:62. Each child of God should realize that the Lord's work shall be done, with or without their cooperation. To renege is to disobey and brings with it a bitter-sweet entrance into the presence of the Lord. It will be sweet to know one is safely home at last, but bitter to realize without reward.

Those who will cooperate with the Lord need to be controlled and empowered by His Spirit. They must be lead by the Holy Spirit, so that when He convenes a meeting at the right time He can plant a seed of truth at the right moment. The child of God that is not lead by the Spirit will seize any opportunity to speak a word of truth, but it will not be in the Spirit. His words will be heard, but not heeded, for the heart is not prepared or no longer prepared; so he speaks too soon or too late. They that imagine they should preach the gospel to every one do err, and bring themselves into bondage and maybe trouble. The great commission requires every child of God to go forth intent to preach the gospel to every one, and do so, as allowed of God.

Preaching the word requires discernment. One must discern the leading of the Spirit in order to know the right time and place to communicate the goodness of God. There are many of God's people engaged in visiting hospitals and prisons, intent on preaching the gospel, and they claim this is their ministry. In doing so, they are taking advantage of ones circumstances, their physical infirmity and mental inactivity and 'corner them' so to speak. There is no need for the Spirit of God to constrain them to listen; and if the Spirit of Christ is not there, then it is all in vain. There is no record in the word of God of a special ministry to the sick or the incarcerated in prisons or the down and outs or to those with mental problems in asylums. Our Lord met such in the way, but left no commandments to establish such institutions. Neither did He establish or give commandment to establish Christian counseling Centres and He definitely did not sanction a special ministry to the devil's disciples, the Russelites, Mormons, and other cults. Such ministries can be used by the devil to side-track the children of God into bypass meadows where they have bypassed the work God has ordained for them and engaged in unprofitable exploits that not only waste God given time but also God given finances.

One brother in his naivety tried to extend his door to door work to ministering to down and outs, alcoholics and drug addicts. The brethren recognized his efforts by praying for his protection and blessing, and were quick to praise him. Our Lord was quick to draw to his attention that he was spending more time chauffeuring around these down and outs to meetings and spending no time on the doors doing the Lord's work. He had to get down to the real business of serving the Lord lawfully as laid down in the word of God and had to get down on his knees to acknowledge his failure. That same brother later remarked saying - how strange it is that in all his years evangelising from door to door, that only one young sister offered to pray for him, but when one engages in such dubious work then all will enjoin it. Yet there is no need, for the enemy will never oppose such work. But the moment one steps forth to evangelise from door to door, he will suffer persecution. Does not nature tell one, that the god of this world will not let his captives go easily.

There will be opposition.

# Righteousness Opposed
# by the devil

God created the heavens and earth and all that is therein, and God saw everthing that He had made, and, behold it was very good. Since it is right to do good then God did right in creating all things for His pleasure. He did right in creating man in His own likeness to live in loving fellowship with Himself for ever as sons of God conformed to the likeness of His only begotten Son, the Lord Jesus Christ. God has been doing right to man since the creation, and the whole world is full of His righteousness. God did right in creating angels to worship and serve God, and to be spirits sent forth to minister for them who shall be heirs of salvation.

There was one, the anointed cherub who was perfect in his ways from the day that he was created, till iniquity was found in him. His heart was lifted up because of his beauty, and his wisdom corrupted by reason of his brightness. He was Lucifer, son of the morning, puffed up with pride, declared his will saying – "I will ascend into heaven, I will exalt my throne above the stars of God: I will sit also upon the mount of the congregation, in the sides of the north: I will ascend above the heights of the clouds; I will be like the most High." Isa.14:13-14. He became known as Satan when God cast him and a host of angels that fell for his ways out of heaven.

As God seeks to do that which is good and right to man, Satan the chief of the fallen angels being hostile to everything good, will devise different ways to stop Him. He will oppose God doing that which is good and right to His people. Then he will oppose the child of God being used to do that which is good and right. Finally he will oppose His creation accepting the goodness of God.

The first man and his helpmate enjoyed the blessing of God whilst in all innocence they lived by faith in close fellowship with God. Satan intent on breaking that fellowship and deny God blessing His people set about to deceive them into unbelief. Being the most gifted of creatures he cunningly targeted the weaker vessel to beguile into doubting the will of God. The man having fallen more in love for the creature than the creator, fell for her prompting which lead to both their down fall and loss of blessing. Many a brother, that showed much promise of being used by God, has fallen to the unwise promptings of his mate and was lead away from God's path and away from blessing.

One such brother with a zeal for the things of God married a sister with a natural gift for singing. The devil beguiled her into thinking that she could be more greatly used by ministering to the people of God through her gift. Her husband consented to her vain imagining. Whilst she waxed strong in her own zeal to entertain, that brother's zeal for the Lord waned. Setting aside the word of God they wandered into a fellowship of believers and unbelievers and away from blessing.

Job was not such an one. When smitten with sore boils from his foot unto his crown, his wife prompted him to curse God and die. He realized that she spoke as one of the foolish women, for such devilish counsel would have ended his life and his service for the Lord. In his flesh he would see God, but not as his redeemer. Instead, Job did not sin with his lips. Truly he feared displeasing God.

Our Lord came into the world to do the will of God, and did say "I delight to do thy will O my God." Psalm 40:8. He did always those things that please the Father, and it pleased Him to consecrate Himself to fulfilling all righteousness, and it pleased the Father, for He did declare – "this is my beloved Son in whom I am well pleased," 2Pet.1:17, and it pleased the Holy Spirit to lead Him into the wilderness to prove that He could not be tempted of evil. There He was subjected to the severest tempting at the hands of the devil, under the most adverse conditions. He suffered, being tempted, yet was without sin. The devil tempted Him to set aside the word of God and act independent of the Father. Our Lord answered and said, "it is written, man shall not live by bread alone, but by every word that proceedeth out of the mouth of God." Math.4:4.

This is a law of life that one must obey in order to abide in fellowship with the Lord and enjoy blessing from God. This is a law that the devil would have one take lightly. He does not want one to take earnest heed to the word of God. He would have man let slip the promises and commandments of God that he might slip away from close fellowship with the Lord and out of blessing.

One brother disobeyed this law of life to his cost. He set aside the guideline "be ye not unequally yoked together with unbelievers." 2Cor.6:14. He married an unbeliever and shortly afterwards she gave birth to a son. Within months she put him away and her secret lover moved in to live with her. Even though that brother was denied access to his son he had to pay for his maintenance, and he was denied the privilege and blessing of raising up his son in the nurture of the Lord. Whilst his wife lived he was not free to marry another. He was further tempted to set aside the word of God and he married again. In doing so he slipped further away from the Lord and became prey for the devil. Those that were not of faith knew that he did wrong. In doing so he had given place for them to reproach him. He had also given place for Satan to seize him and devour his testimony, and thwart the righteousness of God.

God in loving kindness seeks to bless His people and work all things together for their good. All things include the evil things in addition to the good things. Truly Job did say – "what? shall we receive good at the hand of God, and shall we not receive evil?" Job 2:10, and "Yet man is born unto trouble, as the sparks fly upward I would seek unto God, and unto God would I commit my cause Which doeth great things and unsearchable; marvelous things without number: who giveth rain upon the earth, and sendeth waters upon the fields: To set up on high those that be low; that those which mourn may be exalted to safety." Job 5:7-11.

As the rain falls upon the just and the unjust so also trouble falls upon all. When the evil that troubles a soul prevails, he has a problem. The natural man will do that which comes naturally to him. He will try to understand the problem and trust himself to solve it. But he that has been made wise unto salvation will wisely trust the Lord with all his heart and lean not unto his own understanding. However there are children of God, that when some dread accident strikes them a blow they do not commit their cause unto God but worry, fret and demand. They don't realize that things just don't happen to children of God they are part of a wonderful plan; the trials, the troubles, the reverses, the sorrows, the rod are strokes of the Great Sculptor's hand. They are sent to chasten that soul and build him up in doing that which is good and right, and exalt him safely above doing that which is wrong and evil. We must not despise the chastening of the Lord, nor faint when we are rebuked of Him –"for whom the Lord loveth he chasteneth, and scourgeth every son whom He receiveth." Heb.12;5, 6. "Behold, happy the man whom God correcteth: therefore despise not thou the chastening of the Almighty." Job 5:17.

God will exercise each child of God unto righteousness and being omniscient knows how to do so. He knows how to perfect that which belongs to

Himself. He knew how to perfect the experience of the Righteous One. "Though he were a Son, yet learned he obedience by the things which he suffered; And being made perfect, he became the author of eternal salvation unto all them that obey him." Heb.5:8-9. "For in that he himself hath suffered being tempted, he is able to succour them that are tempted." Heb.2:18.

Doubting our Lord's reliance on the Father the devil determined to have Him act independent of the Father, took Him to a high and lofty place, and tempted Him to prove that God will provide for Him. Our Lord said unto him, "it is written again - thou shalt not tempt the Lord thy God." Math.4:7. This is another law of life. The devil will tempt man to put the Lord to the test. Appealing to the lust of the flesh and the desires of the mind he will entice him to buy a car or house without money. He will beguile him into imaging that this is a step of faith. It is not of faith. It is of financing. It is sin. It is the sin of presumption - presuming that the Lord will provide the payments. He must learn and obey this second law of life.

There was one of whom God did say – "I have found David, a man after mine own heart, who shall fulfill all my will." He was a Godly man, who inquired of the Lord, encouraged himself in the Lord, and declared that "the Lord saveth not with the sword and spear" 1Sam.17:47. The devil knows that God will have His people count on Him to fight and win their battles and not to count on their own resources. Yet he succeeded in provoking that one into numbering the people. Today he tempts the people of God to count on their own resources. He will have them use their own natural abilities to persuade, woo and win souls. In doing so he is seeking to seduce them into working in their own strength and thus render to nought the righteousness of God.

The devil, fully determined to have our Lord act independent of the Father and doubting His love for the Father took Him up into an exceedingly high mountain and tempted Him with the offer of great glory if He would renounce His love for the Father. But that the world may know that He loved the Father, and as He hath given Him commandment, even so He did, and He commanded the devil, "get thee hence, satan; for it is written thou shalt worship the Lord, thy God and Him only shalt thou serve." Math.4:10. Our Lord sought to glorify the Father and that He did in love for the Father, and succeeded against all evil.

The devil will test man's love for God by appealing to his love of self and of glory. He will tempt man to think more highly of himself than he ought. Then he will tempt him to make a name for himself by having him take every opportunity to perform as a preacher or teacher. But it is all vanity. It lacketh love. His audience remains unmoved. It profiteth nothing. It is not of God.

Job was a man that was perfect and one that feared God and eschewed evil. Of all the men of the east he had great possessions, that which he had received from above. The devil did target his heart hoping that his possessions might possess him. He took from him that which was close to his heart, his family and his wealth, hoping that would turn him against God. But Job's heart being perfect in love for God, instead of falling for the devices of the devil, he fell down upon the ground and worshipped God saying – "naked came I out of my mother's womb, and naked shall I return. The Lord gave, and the Lord hath taken away; blessed be the name of the Lord." Job.1:21. The servant of God must learn the third law of life – "thou shalt worship the Lord, thy God, and Him only shalt thou serve."Math.4;12.

Our Lord in not yielding to the Satan's tempting, proved that He could not be tempted to sin. He also manifested His power over the devil, and when He told him to be gone - he obeyed. The devil then went forth, not accepting defeat; he was not distressed, not even disappointed and definitely not deterred, but definitely more determined to stop the work of God. Realizing he could not succeed with the Lord, he then sought to hinder the work of God doing good through His people. He knew the right one to attack; the one quick to crow about himself saying – "though all men shall be offended because of thee, yet will I never be offended." Math.26:33. Our Lord said unto him, "verily I say unto thee that this night before the cock crow, thou shalt deny me thrice." Math.26:34

Our Lord knew that Satan hath desired him, that he may sift him as wheat. The devil desired to put an end to Peter's service, by separating him from the Lord. Our Lord prayed for Peter, and knew that his pride would be wounded and that he would be converted from seeking his own glory, for He knew that godly sorrow would work repentance and through his experience he could strengthen the brethren.

Peter's experience offers some comfort to those of God's people who have backsliden through being puffed up with self. It manifests more so the mercy of God and later the grace of God in using him to open the keys of the kingdom of heaven. Nevertheless it dishonoured God and left a mark on Peter's testimony. He was restored within three days to be used mightily. Now there is no assurance that a backslider will be restored so quickly and further used, but there is one thing assured that it will leave its mark on his service, for it has been well said that a '*wounded bird never flies so high*'. In order to safe guard against falling for the devil's device of separating from the Lord and His people, one should abide in the Lord and His word.

The devil will have his demons oppress and persecute the child of God that will live righteously, soberly and godly in this world. He had a damsel mock Paul so much that it interfered with his preaching the gospel. Being grieved he commanded the evil spirit to come out off her. When her masters saw the hope of their income gone they immediately caught Paul and Silas, and dragged them into the market place to make a show of them and accuse them of troubling the people. They beat them and cast them into prison, hoping that would put an end to preaching the way of salvation. But, it resulted in the devil outsmarting himself; for what he meant for evil, God meant for good. God used Paul's time in jail to convene a meeting between him and the jailer regarding faith in Christ, and to show the way of salvation unto him and his household. All believed and were born again into the family of God.

God having set aside one unto belief of the truth, will use the word of God to indoctrinate that one with the will of God, reprove him of doing that which is not the will of God, correct him and instruct him in the right way to do right. He will lead him into all truth and the ways of righteousness. The devil knows that for the child of God to do right the right way he must obey the Lord's command through the Apostle Paul "be filled with the Spirit." Eph.5:17. He will seek to keep the child of God in the dark as to this truth. This he has been doing down through the years and has succeeded in hindering it being taught. Subsequently many of God's people never come to the knowledge of this truth, and so they spend the time of their sojourn here feeling their way through life, never knowing the leading of the Spirit and the way of righteousness.

The Spirit of truth will lead the people of God into all truth. He will not lead them into untruth or into speaking lies in hypocrisy. The devil knowing that God will definitely not take control of any one that does, will have his demons beguile would be teachers into corrupting the word of God to mislead the people of God into embracing false doctrines, thus rendering them unacceptable for use as coworkers together with the Lord in the ministry of righteousness.

Just as the devil would have believers blind to the truth of ministration, he will have those that are unbelievers blind to the truth of salvation. He will tempt them to indulge in things that God never meant for them. He tempted a young girl of 17 yrs. to try the 'bubbly' champagne. Having opened her up to trying new things, he then captivated her with the taste of stronger beverages. She reached the point of no return. She had become his captive. She married a publican (tavern owner). There was no shortage of wine and strong wine and there was whisky galore. No doubt he meant to do her and her husband evil. But God meant to do them good. In His time He delivered them both from the power of darkness and translated them into the kingdom of His dear Son.

The Lord God said "Behold all souls are mine." Ezek.18:4. In loving kindness for those that are not of the household of faith, God will move toward man in order to do him a favour that he does not deserve, that of presenting to him the truth (the word of God) that He might make him wise unto salvation. There are those that would hear the word of God, but the devil will seek to prevent them. When Paul and Barnabas had gone through the isle of Cyprus they came to Paphos where they found a certain sorcerer, a false prophet, a Jew, whose name was Barjesus. He was aptly named, for he did seek to bar Jesus from doing good through His servants to one who was a prudent man, that desired to hear the word of God.

This device of using another to do his evil deeds to oppose the will of God, he still uses today. The terrorist that plants the bomb is not the one that plans the bombing. The policeman that stops one preaching from house to house is not the one that stoops to complain. When the personal worker is engaging one in conversation regarding faith in Christ, the voice of one unseen can be heard calling that one away.

Then there are those who have heard the word of God, and the wicked one will come and attempt to take away the word of God. He will succeed with those that will gladly receive the word of God, yet casually (by the way). Such are left with their feelings to direct them into a way that appears right unto them but the way thereof is the way of death. Broad is the way that leads to destruction and many there be on it that have heard the word of God and casually received it, and never hearkened to it.

Then again there are those that have heard the word of God, the enemy would come feigning to be messengers of light, ministers of righteousness. Such are false prophets of the cults and sow tares (seeds of untruth) in that soul to mislead him into a way that is not the way of righteousness. Quite often, the servant of God will happen to meet one who God has sanctified unto the hearing of the truth, and as he seeks to be faithful, he will find that false prophets have been visiting that home and sowing their tares. Does he try to root out the false teaching? Nay, he may root up also the wheat. He continues to present truth upon truth, knowing that truth will always expose untruth, and he that is sanctified unto belief of the truth will gather the wheat and store it. Having fulfilled his mission, the servant of God may help his subject to discern a false prophet, by showing him that such deny the bodily resurrection of Jesus Christ our Lord and Saviour.

The devil knows that God justified the Son of God through His bodily resurrection, and will seek to deny it at all costs, for therein is the power of the Lord God, who not only claimed that He had power to lay down His life but He had also power to take it again. Furthermore therein lies the power of the gospel, for through the resurrection of our Lord, He is able to save to the uttermost all that come unto God through Him seeing He ever liveth to make intercession for them. Satan will use anybody and any body of people to deny the resurrection of the Lord.

When Paul and Silas passed through Amphipolis and Apollonia, they came to Thessalonica, where was a synagogue, of the Jews. Paul, as his manner was, went in unto them, and three sabbath days reasoned with them out of the scriptures, opening and alleging that Christ must needs have suffered, and risen again from the dead; and that this Jesus, whom he preached unto them was Christ. There was power in his preaching for some believed and consorted with Paul and Silas; and of the devout Greeks a great multitude, and of the chief women not a few. But when the Jews who believed not, moved with envy, took unto them certain lewd fellows of the baser sort, and gathered a company, and set all the city in an uproar, and assaulted the house of Jason, to bring them out to the people. They were intending to put an end to such preaching.

The devil's opposition to the gospel has not changed down through the years. Today he is still using all kinds of people to oppose the preaching of the gospel. As the servant of God goes forth in a neighbourhood, he does not go unnoticed. Those strongly steeped in religion will through envy be moved to incite others to draw nigh and interrogate him as to his person and purpose. They seek not a reason but an excuse for them to threaten or lay hands on him. He knowing that he must not withhold the truth to avoid hostility and that they could have no power except it be given them from above, must quickly discern whether it is the will of God for him to continue or to move on as the Spirit would lead him.

Having failed to stop a servant's mouth and being determined to oppose the righteousness of God, he will then try to stop the servant. One such brother having diligently preached the gospel for some 15 yrs sought to do a young man a favour by lending him his car. The enemy seduced him into attacking the servant. He grabbed him by the throat and set about to choke him. The sentence of death was upon him. Truly the devil meant it for evil. But God meant it for good. He delivered that servant and used him to sow more abundantly in the years that followed. The young man married and about 10 years later his wife was tempted into adultery and divorce. What the devil meant for evil God meant for good. He used the tragedy to bring that young man to repentance and into relationship with Himself. Today both men are coworkers with the Lord and can be seen going from house to house teaching and preaching Jesus Christ.

Truly the child of God must needs realize that we wrestle not against flesh and blood, but against principalities, against powers, against the rulers of the darkness of this world, against spiritual wickedness in high places. Each of us must put on the whole armour of God that we may be able to withstand in the evil day, and having done all to stand. We need also to be filled with the Holy Spirit in order to discern the wiles of the devil and war against the enemy.

Being well equipped and prepared to fulfil all righteousness we servants of God go forth to live according to the word of God, and not according to the course of this world.

# Righteousness Opposed by the world

From its beginning the world has been on a course away from God, and from His authority. This movement has been gaining momentum down through the ages and will reach its consummation when the inhabitants will not have Him rule over them, and will resist all rule, and will be as those without a king; they will fulfil the imaginations of the thoughts of their heart. It will be as it was in the day of Noah, when the people did eat, they drank, they married; they were given in marriage until the day that Noah entered into the Ark, and the floods came and destroyed them. Instead of using their God given intellect to gather knowledge of their creator, people go to and fro seeking knowledge of the creature, and are become vain in their imagining, and their hearts love the lie rather than the truth.

Professing themselves to be wise, they become fools, for they leave God out of their lives. They love not God or their neighbour, but themselves. They become covetous and seek after position, power and possessions. They seek their own. Most would seek a good reputation, and would feign being righteous and would claim being affiliated with a religious organization. They have a form of godliness, but deny the power thereof.

Some will seek to join the people of God in their work unto the Lord in their neighbourhood. They do so hoping to enlarge their own church. Just as they would compromise their own beliefs they would expect the brethren to do likewise. But to do so would require disobeying the word of God, and that would be sin. To permit infidels to share in the Lord's work would only weaken and bring it to nought. The believer has no part with infidels, and must not be unequally yoked with them. 2Cor.6:16,17. We must take the same stance as the Jews who returned under Zerubbabel's leadership to build the temple and determined- "we ourselves together will build unto the Lord God." Ezra 4:3.

Such nominal christians despise the brethren and with great indignation mock them saying – *'They think they are the only ones that are right' - 'They think they are the only ones going to heaven' - 'They are doing this work to increase their membership'. 'What they are doing will come to nought.* When this fails to discourage the children of God they will solicit the help of others to frustrate them. They will appeal to local governments to legislate against door to door evangelism claiming it is an annoyance and an intrusion of privacy. Those with a mind to work will continue to do so in spite of such opposition, whilst continuing to be subject to the powers that be. On perceiving that this has failed to stop the work, they will conspire with others to physically force the brethren to stop. The people of God must not retaliate. Realizing that the weapons of our warfare are not carnal, but mighty through God to the pulling down of strong holds, we will do as Nehemiah and look to the Lord in prayer.

The people having tasted of the luxuries of affluence are greedy for all that life has to offer. They will indulge in sumptuous living unto gluttony and obesity. Their belly becomes their god. They no longer eat to live but now live to eat. Many will afford the high cost of having food prepared for them. Not only is the world guilty of surfeiting, but also many of the people of God.

Not only does the world crave after food, but it indulges in winebibbing. Wine has a numbing effect on man's body and a stupefying effect on his mind. The more consumed, the more will be its deadening effect on that person and the less conscious will he be of what is right or wrong, and he care less about it's lasting effect; and the less he will kick against the pricks. The devil has used it to dupe many souls to remain in the dark so that the light of the glory of the gospel of Jesus Christ can not shine into their hearts and they remain in a stupor all their lives until they open their eyes in hades.

There are those, who in times past were nobodies and followed the course of this world, and are now the children of God, and are being delivered from the power of darkness and sinful habits. They return to the beggarly elements (Gal4:9), and walk after the flesh. They will follow the course of this world, and imbibe the devil's potion, which leads them to further imbibing of the principles and practices of this world. Such deluded Christians seek to justify their wine imbibing by saying that our Lord was a winebibber. They fail to behold that it was the people who described Him as such, and they further fail to behold that portion of scripture ends thus – "wisdom is justified of her children." Math.11:19. The wise child will not be filled with wine, but will be filled with the Holy Spirit.

The child of God who would unwisely excuse himself into imbibing wine should realize he is defiling the temple of the Holy Spirit. He is sinning against God and God will not use one who does evil to himself to do good to others. He would do well to realize that every one who bends the elbow to down the devil's potion is a potential alcoholic. He should also realize that the devil has seduced him into opposing the righteousness of God.

The world is marrying and given in marriage, just as it did in the days of Noah. Since then man has been increasing in knowledge and improvising, so that he has developed new excuses for breaking the marriage bond. Today marriages are being annulled in the courts of all countries on grounds unheard of in the times of Noah, and Lot.

As the flesh lusts after that which God never intended, and the laws of the lands relax to accommodate the masses, the world waxes gross in fornication. Each culprit that enjoys the pleasure of his sin, will oppose any attempt to restrict him doing that which pleases him. It does not please him to be reproved. He does not want to be exposed. He loves darkness, rather than light because his deeds are evil. He will not come near one who speaks the truth. So, the servant of God has got to go to him, and seek to deal with him in truth. He will scoff at the word of God, and scorn those that preach it. So great are his lusts that he does not want to change. He is one of the many that walk after their ungodly lusts, and has not only pleasure in them that do like wise, but will encourage them to do so and together they will stand to oppose the righteousness of God.

There are those who claim to be children of God, that would make them comfortable in their sin. They would try to misconstrue the scriptures to sanction divorce. The word of God teaches **'one man one wife for life'** and God has ordered it so. Putting aside this truth in order to put away one's partner creates problems. So great that many will not pay the price to be converted. Those that aided and abetted them in their divorcing cannot help them in their problem. They can only share in their sin.

Marrying and giving in marriage is creeping into assembly life. Men have risen and are still rising among the people of God, speaking perverse things to draw away disciples after themselves. They know that the people like to hear some new thing, and they teach this new thing of divorce for the people of God. The child of God that falls for such teaching and falls into divorcing his God given partner, when rebuked for his evil deed, will relay the blame unto the so called servants of God.

Both teacher and doer of this evil deed are guilty of this sin, which will separate them from fellowship with God and the people of God in a lawful assembly. It will also rob them of the privilege of being used by God to do that which is good and right to others, and so the work of the Lord is hindered.

Also as it was in the days of Lot they did eat, they did drink, they bought, they sold, they planted, they built, so it is in these days prior to our Lord's return. Increase in family income makes it easier for people to afford the necessities of life and to taste its luxuries. People buy houses to live in, and as their value increases, they see the opportunity to sell for profit, and seize it. The eye of man is never satisfied, and he seeks further opportunities and capitalizes on his gains. Today the whole world is buying and selling where possible, not because of need but for want. They don't buy a house that will do them for good, but one that will do them a good turn. They don't confine their profit making to buying and selling houses, but have progressed to taking chances on buying and selling stocks and shares. The people are busy buying and selling houses, cars, boats and whatever they possess, so that their possessions are possessing them. They have no time for God. They have no time to seek after God, no time to stop to hear what God has for them, and so they prevent God doing them good.

The people of God would be as the nations and buy houses which hath foundations whose builder and maker is man. Unlike God's earthly people that journeyed to the promised land and each day pitched their tent a day nearer home, some of God's heavenly people being short-sighted, and far from home have settled for the ways of the people of the land and dwell in their wood paneled houses. Just as it is difficult to pick up a house and pitch it a day nearer home, it is difficult to pick the people of God out of the world. They have lost their pilgrim character. They have lost their zeal for the things of God. Instead of occupying themselves with the building of the house of God they are occupied with building their own house. Haggai though he were dead yet liveth his words – "is it time for you, Oh ye, to dwell in your cieled houses and this house (of God) waste?" Now, therefore, thus saith the Lord of hosts: consider your ways.

# Righteousness Opposed
# by the flesh

The child of God should not only consider his own ways but also the ways of others. He should realize that man being born separated from God is dead to the things of God and his spirit is disposed to declension and deadness, and his body is bound to physical death. He seeks not after God; consequently he lacks knowledge of God. He is of the world and speaketh of the world. He knows only that which concerns himself. He thinks more highly of himself than he should, and imagines that he is better than the next. Accordingly, he despises instruction. So, when one comes to him with good news, he automatically suspects that he is going to hear correction and the need to change. This he resents, and since man is bent on doing wrong, he will naturally resist changing to do right. Hence man is disposed to opposing God doing him good. He opposes the righteousness of God.

When the giant Goliath came out and beheld David, he looked down upon him with contempt, feeling he was not worthy of his attention. Yet he did attend to the fact that he was armed with staves. The Philistine cursed David by his gods. So, it is with each of those to whom we would seek to do good and communicate the goodness of God. He will scornfully look down upon the servant of God, considering him not worthy of his attention. Yet he does attend to the fact that he is armed with the Bible. But fearing reproof and correction and feeling vexed that such an one should dare approach to correct him, he will curse within himself that servant. He will unconsciously go on the defensive and take up arms for battle. The more puffed up with pride, the more vigorous will be his defence. Those full of pride will dig in for battle, they are the indignant and are extreme. On the other extreme there are those that are least puffed up with pride, they are the least active. They are as those that sleep. They are the indolent. Subsequently, disposition will vary according to pride of spirit, and manifest itself in attitudes varying from indolency to indignancy. Man's disposition is a giant obstacle that stands in the way of God doing right to him, and must be changed; it must be displaced.

Man must be stopped in his tracks to listen, and then the giant disposition to resist the truth must be rendered powerless in order for that one to realize that without God, all is vanity. The big ego must be broken down, slain and then replaced with a desire to know truth planted in his heart. The Lord God wrestled with Jacob in order to conquer and change his disposition yet he prevailed, and He had to displace a hip joint in order to render him powerless and make him realize that he wrestled with one greater than himself and one that could bless him. Truly, our Lord is greater than Jacob, and He who conquered him and changed his name, also changed him, and only He can conquer the unregenerate and change them and change their name and is not ashamed to call them brethren. The Lord in doing good to His creation, in wondrous grace deigns to use His people as channels of mercy, to wrestle with and conquer the spirits of such giants that will come out against God. As they stand before us servants of God, we must not forget the words of our Lord – "that without Me, ye can do nothing" John 15:5, and so we must not dare try in our own strength to conquer such giants, but rejoice with this confidence that "in all things we are more than conquerors through Him that loved us."Rom.8:37. .

David fearing that one stone would be insufficient, bowed down and choose five stones from the bed of the river (brook or stream). They were not too big and heavy to sling or too small and light to bounce off to no effect. They were not hewn out by the hands of man. They had no sharp edges that would pierce the giant and plunge him to his death. They were smooth stones shaped by God and suited for David, but only one was sufficient for God achieving His purpose of staving, stunning, and stopping the giant without slaying him. The servant of God would be wise to get similar stones that he can sling and which God will use to stop his subject. They wont be sharp and cutting statements that will pierce and cut to the heart and cut short the meeting and cut off the opportunity to do good. They won't be got in a cosy arm chair, but bowed to the will of God, the servant of God will get that which he seeks in the main stream of life.

The vast majority of people, the servant of God will meet are ignorant of their need; they know not God, nor the truth of salvation. When asked the question *Can you see the need to get saved ?* They will answer - *no, I don't!* The servant of God, will seek to show them that need, and tell them of God's provision. If that person is humble he will listen to learn, and hopefully he will be poor enough to accept the truths he hears, and be made wise unto salvation. If, he is not humble and does not want to hear, then the servant of God must discern the nature of the disposition, deal with him accordingly.

Now, there are many giants in this land and they will come out unto the servant of God with a sword, a shield, and a spear. The sword he will use to cut to pieces one's argument, his presentation of the truth. He will seek to slay the servant of God with the wisdom of man 1Cor.1:21. The shield he will use to hold back the truth in unrighteousness. He will try to discredit the word of God, saying that the Bible was written by man; it is full of contradictions; it is only a book. The spear he will use to persecute the servant. Failing to discredit the word of God, he will then pin point his attack at the servant of God.

It is remarkable that, just as their defence begins with the big 'I', each of their names begin with 'I'.

(1) **The Giant of Indolence** is disposed to idleness, inactivity, love of ease, wanting no bother, no trouble. and despises anyone that would disturb him in his listless life. He is too idle to do anything. He does not take kindly a servant of God coming to show him another way to live. When asked the introductory question, he will sluggishly answer - *I'm easy man, don't bother me with such things.* The servant of God may rush at him the saying - *You may be at ease in time, but will you be at ease in eternity ?* This has troubled some, enough to want to hear more.cf Lk.12:16-21

(2) **The Giant of Insincerity** is disposed to not being serioius. This is manifest in him saying one thing and thinking another. He will agree with everything the servant of God says and will answer *'aye, sir'* to every question, and when asked *'do you see the need to get saved'* will automatically answer *'aye'*. The servant of God might give him something serious to consider by firing at - *do you believe there is God,* then *do you believe that God will punish the world for it's evil* and then *unless you repent and believe the gospel He will punish you.*cf Math.21:18-32.

(3) **The Giant of Indifference** is disposed to carelessness as manifest in his lack of interest and concern for others. He cares little about the welfare of others and even his

own, and he cares less about changing. He even fears the trouble of changing. When questioned about the need to get saved he shrugs - *'I'm not interested in that.'* The servant of God might stave him by saying - *you would be if you knew what lies before you.* This has troubled some to want to know. He will then proceed to show him the indifference of the Gadarenes and how their fear lead them to rejecting the saviour and to eternal torment. (Luke 8:26-39, and Luke 16:19-31).

(4) **The Giant of Industry** is disposed to pursuing a means to an end. He busies himself with all kinds of pursuits but mainly that of laying up for himself much goods that he might take it easy in his latter years. He is too busy with no time for God. To the introductory question, he will quickly answer - *I'm too busy.* Once again, one doesn't have much time to stun him, so the servant of God can with the help of the Holy Spirit direct the following stave at him - *it is wise to be busy, but unwise to be too busy and have no time for God.* If, he is the giant that should fall that day, then he'll hear on. The servant of God will proceed to show him the folly of two such men in Luke 12:16-20, 16:19-31.

(5) **The Giant of Indulgence** is disposed to indulging in the desires of the flesh and that which God never intended for him. One will recognise him by such apologising as *I like a wee drink, and a little nightlife, and there are lots of good things in this world that I enjoy.* The servant of God will sling at him - *A little*

*folly now and then fetters the best of men. What shall your end be if you die fettered and fixed in your ways?* Recall to him Lot's wife. She lost her husband, and she lost her life. She lost her lot. She died fixed in her ways - a warning to all who would indulge and would not repent. Gen.19:15-26.

(6) **The Giant of Indecision** is disposed to wavering. He is reluctant to make decisions and to answer questions. He will avoid having to answer questions by not giving the servant of God the opportunity to ask any. When asked the introductory question, he will quickly quip - *I don't want to discuss such things now.* The messenger is given almost no time to operate; he has only time to sling the stave, *God has afforded you now, and it may be now or never.* To those stopped in their track, the servant will proceed to show them that it is God that convenes meetings and the folly of Felix in putting off to a convenient time that which he should have done that day. Acts 24:22-27.

(7) **The Giant of Infatuation** is disposed to thinking more highly of himself than he ought and is unwilling to accept the counsel of others. He is too full of himself to give ear to another. When asked the introductory question, he will very quickly assert saying - *I'm all right*, thinking that it is the start and finish of the encounter. One will very quickly counter by saying - *that is what you think you are, but God knows that you are a sinner condemned. Do you know that?* The servant

of God may proceed to show him from Luke 18:10-14., the folly of seeing the good and not the evil in oneself and not seeing the need to fear God.

(8) **The Giant of Impudence** is disposed to being foolhardy in presuming that he is right. When asked the introductory question he will answer '*I feel that God will accept me.*' One might fire at him - *You do err not knowing the scriptures. You may feel your way now, but if you don't find the right way in time you will feel the wrath of God in eternity.*

(9) **The Giant of Irrationality** is disposed to being unreasonable. He is too witless to consider. He will be recognized by such judgmental sarcastic answers to the introductoy question as - *I know them that are good living, and I wouldn't do the things they do.* The servant will fire at him. *If you are right they are wrong. They are hypocrites. But, remember there are no hypocrites in heaven; they all shall have their part in the lake which burneth with fire and brimstone. But, unless you repent, you shall likewise perish.* Math.11:16-19.

(10) **The Giant of Insolence** is disposed to haughtiness, arrogancy manifest in defiance, scorn, and impertinence.

He knows about creation, and the promise of His coming, but he also knows his lusts and does not want to change, and is determined to continue. Thinking himself to be wise, he will brazenly scoff at the word of God and scorn the servant of God. When asked the introductory question he will answer - *I know the Bible and what it says about His coming again, but it hasn't happened.* One might stun him with the stave - *you may know a lot about the Bible, but you don't know the God of the Bible, and if you don't obey the gospel of the Lord Jesus Christ before you die or before the Lord comes, you will know the wrath of God throughout eternity.* The servant of God may show him prophecy fulfilled, especially in the Lord's first coming and the signs foreshadowing His second coming.

(11) **The Giant of Indebtedness** is too sweet to be wholesome. He is not for real, but he really means to get rid of the servant of God. To the introductory question he will smugly answer - *I thank you for your tract and will read it for you.* One might stave him by saying - *don't thank me, but thank God that you are still alive and have not received your just reward, but have received this opportunity to hear of the goodness of God.*

(12) **The Giant of Indiscretion** is disposed to imprudence and rashness. As one offers a tract he will gladly feign sorrow saying - '*I'm sorry. No*'. One might stave him saying –no need to *sorrow now! Will you be sorry in eternity?*

(13) **The Giant of Infidelity** is disposed to not wanting to believe there is God. He wants to do as he pleases, and does not want to be accountable to anyone. When asked

the intro ductory question, he glories in asserting - *I'm an atheist !*. This is meant to frighten away the servant of God. But he does not run away, but runs at him saying - *You can't prove there is no God but I can prove there is God*. That will stave, stun and stop him. One can easily prove that there is God by fulfilled prophecy, especially that of the death, burial, and resurrection of our Lord cf Ps. 16:10., 1Cor.15:3,4. Only God could have raised Him from the dead !

(14) **The Giant of Indignation** is disposed to disdaining anyone trying to give him counsel. He is much puffed up with pride, presuming himself to be wise, Rom.1:21., he imagines that he is above others in abilities and capabilities. When the servant of God asks him the introductory question, he immediately knows that this visitor comes in the name of the Lord. Fearing reproof and correction, and sensing that the servant is going to tell him something he doesn't want to hear, he will reply saying - 'I *am well able to know God without people like you coming to tell me*' hoping that will slay the servant of God. He will not run from this giant, but will hasten and run at him and sling at him - *a man can receive nothing except it be given him from above and one can only know God by revelation and God deigns to use His own servants to do that.* This stave when directed by the Holy Spirit will smite him, and sink into his head and stun and stop him.

(15) **The Giant of Inveteracy** after prolonged period of sinning against God and doing evil his heart has hardened, and he will not accept truth or any thing pertaining to the things of God. To the introductory question he will snap- '*I don't want to hear*'. The servant of God realizes that such an one's conscience is seared and as he backs off he reasons within himself, that whilst there is life there is hope, and so hoping against hope he will sling - '*You can cut off hearing the word of God in time, but you can't cut of the wrath of God in eternity*'.

The servant of God having staved and stopped whichever giant that he encounters should slay each with the Sword of the Lord, and then proceed to show each the goodness of God.

# Righteousness Opposed by the flesh of the saints

The children of God, having repented and believed the gospel, and having been blessed with every spiritual blessing in the heavenlies in Christ, have privileges and responsibilities. We have the right to do right, that is our right by birth into the family of God. As we journey along the King's highway we will be tested to prove whether we will walk in His way or not. God knows the heart and knows whether we will walk according to the word of God or not, and so this proving is one of us proving to ourselves and not to God. As we journey towards heaven and home, we must take another leap of faith to cross into the place of promised rest, where God will supply our needs and wants. This second crossing is one of consecrating oneself to wholly following the Lord.

The child of God having crossed his Jordan will encounter more obstacles to doing right or rather God doing right through him. These obstacles are big. They are giant dispositions that must be overcome, and these are within, and already have possession of the soul. Each child of God would be wise to take that leap of faith to possess his possessions as soon as he is challenged. He would avoid wandering in the wilderness, knowing what he should have done, yet did not do it. Many years may be needed to prove to that child of God that he is prepared to walk in His law. He will have his Jordan to cross into the promised land of need (milk) and want (honey), and into His rest from all that would disturb the tranquillity of his soul.

The child of God needs to purpose within his heart to do the will of God whatever the cost and be filled with the Spirit of God in order to overcome the giants within, that would hinder him doing the right that God would have him do and receiving his inheritance, yea possessing his possessions. In times past, he was dead in trespasses and sin. He was dead to the things of God and his spirit disposed to declension and deadness. When quickened by the Spirit of God he was made alive unto God. He should have died to self and his love of self should be dead. He should love first and foremost the Lord God, who first loved him and gave Himself for him. However, the old man still abides in the flesh, and if not put to death daily he will seek to establish himself. His love for himself will increase whilst his love for the Lord will decrease and he will drift from his first love. He will do the work of the Lord; even labour with all patience. He will not tolerate them that are evil and will try them that claim to be prophets and prove them false; yet all is without love for the Lord. Infatuated with himself he wants to do the work of God, but not the will of God. He will want to preach to large crowds of people, but not to the individual. He does not want to leave all and go to the uttermost end of the world and be forgotten. Thus the righteousness of God will be hindered.

This **Giant of Infatuation** must be overcome, otherwise he that drifts from his first love, will further drift in his love for what is true and right, and his heart will drift from purposing to wholly following the Lord. His resolve to stand up for the truth and what is right and for the Lord will weaken into indecisiveness, and even though he is enriched by Christ in all utterance and all knowledge, the testimony of Christ is not confirmed in him. He fears man and will compromise the truth to suit his hearers.

This **Giant of Indecision** must be overcome, otherwise the child of God who will not stand up for the truth and what is right and for our Lord will fall for untruth. He will not suffer for the cause of righteousness and will give in under trial and tribulation and he will fall for an easier path and fall for the world of make-believe, which has a form of Godliness but denieth the power thereof. He will sell himself and the truth. He will use gift to profit, position and power. Accordingly he will thirst after fame and fortune and hunger for praise to feed his pride. But he will not hunger and thirst after righteousness. Whilst one indulges in seeking his own glory, he cannot do all for the glory of God. He cannot serve both God and himself.

This **Giant of Indulgence** must be overcome, otherwise the child of God will slip into being too busy and have no time for God. He will not take time to get alone with God in order to ascertain the will of God, so that the little that he does is not a work of faith; his labour will not be of love and there will be no patience of hope in our Lord Jesus Christ. He will be too busy seeking fame, fortune and his own welfare and not that which is needful.

This **Giant of Industry** must be overcome, otherwise the child of God will slip into neglecting the word of God and loosing interest in the things of God and care little about false teaching of others, and care less about confronting them. He that is indifferent to the goodness of God will be indifferent to the need of others.

This **Giant of Indifference** must be overcome, otherwise the child of God will not want to see the urgency of doing good now and will slip into that state where he does not feel like doing the good he should. He feels he can put off until tomorrow what he should do today. Though a child of God he does not behave as one. He no longer has a genuine interest in the things of God, nor a real concern for souls. He will not go forth to work in the vineyard today. There is no fear of God in him. He knows what he should do, but does not want to make a sincere decision to do it today, so rather than decide to serve the Lord, he leaves it to a more convenient time and does nothing now. He knows that the door of opportunity has been opened unto him, yet in not availing himself of the privilege, he has erred, for unknown unto him he has made a decision; he has decided not to decide to serve the Lord.

This **Giant of Insincerity** must be overcome, otherwise the child of God will slip to that place from whence he can slip no further. He has declined to that place of inactivity, where every thing he could do, he feels is too much trouble and not worth the bother, for there is nothing in it for him. There is no glory in personal work as no one can see him perform and praise him, so he takes his ease. He will remain at home in the comfort of his study, and comfort himself with the words of the Psalmist – "blessed is the man that walketh not in the counsel of the ungodly, nor standeth in the way of sinners, nor sitteth in the seat of the scornful. but his delight is in the law of the Lord; and in His law doth he meditate day and night." Psalm 1:1-2. Truly God will bless him, but God has ordained us unto good works that others may be blessed through us, like a fruitful bough by a well whose branches run over the wall and bringeth forth his fruit in season. This is difficult to do while one is meditating in his study. There is the danger of over meditating; one may fall over to sleep and time slip quickly by without having done the will of God, only to slip out into the presence of the Lord without receiving that - *well done my good and faithful servant*, and then to give account of himself unto God.

This **Giant of Inactivity** must be overcome, for such an one though he liveth yet is dead. He is dead in his love for the Lord; dead in faith in the Lord using him, and dead is his hope in the Lord coming for him. Dead is his desire to do good and dead is his thinking, for though he has increased with goods and has need of nothing, and thinks he is rich, he is not rich in eternal blessings from God. He is not rich in love, joy, peace and all that abounds unto happiness but is wretched and miserable and poor and blind that he cannot see afar off. He cannot see that he is naked with no righteousnesses with which to be clothed throughout eternity. Knowing the time, that now it is high time for such an elect one of God to awake out of his sleep: for now is his and our salvation nearer than when we first believed. The night is far spent, the day is at hand: let us therefore cast off the works of darkness, and let us put on the armour of light, and put on the Lord Jesus Christ. According as His divine power hath given unto us all things that pertain unto life and godliness, through the knowledge of Him that hath called us to glory and virtue: "whereby are given unto us exceedingly great and precious promises: that by these we might be partakers of the divine nature, having escaped the corruption that is in the world through lust. And beside this, giving all diligence, add to our faith virtue; and to virtue knowledge."2Pet.1:4-5

These giants must be overcome in order to possess our possessions that have been promised to us. Only those that have another spirit and who want to wholly follow the Lord will overcome these giants. Now, every child of God has another spirit, but does every child of God want to wholly follow the Lord. The heart of the matter is the heart. Is it the desire of your heart to wholly follow the Lord ?

If it be so, there shall be reward!

# Righteousness Rewarded

Our Lord Jesus Christ, when in the body prepared for Him, did comfort those who would follow Him in fulfilling all righteousness, by saying -

"blessed the poor in spirit - for theirs is the kingdom of heaven.

blessed they that mourn, for they shall be comforted.

blessed the meek for they shall inherit the earth.

blessed they who hunger and thirst after righteousness for they shall be filled.

blessed the merciful for they shall obtain mercy.

blessed the pure in heart fot they shall see God.

blessed the peacemakers for they shall be called the children of God.

blessed they who are persecuted for righteousness sake for theirs is the kingdom of heaven.

> blessed are ye when men shall revile
> you and persecute you, and shall say all
> manner of evil against you falsely for
> my sake, rejoice and be exceedingly glad
> for great is your reward in heaven, for so
> persecuted they the prophets who were
> before you."Math.5:3-12.

They who speak forth for God shall be humble and poor in spirit, and they shall be comforted when they mourn and shall be kept meek to possess that which the earth has to offer without it possessing them. They shall not walk according to the course of this world. But shall hunger and thirst to do right at all times, and their lives will be filled with opportunities, and God will be further merciful and enable them to show mercy to others. With pure hearts, free of imperfections and perfect with God they shall see and know the Lord. Such will follow peace with all, for they are ambassadors of Him who is the Prince of Peace, and will suffer persecution for the cause of righteousness. They will do right with the right mind, by the right means, for the right motive, in the right manner, and they will rejoice and be exceedingly glad, for great will be their reward in heaven.

God has given to each of His own the Spirit of His Son who enables us to love God, and to do right the right way. We are well equipped to be able ministers of the new covenant of the Spirit; "for we have not the spirit of fear but of love, of power and of a sound mind." 2Tim.1:7. Seeing then, we have this ministry of the Holy

Spirit doing right through us to His creation, we who have received mercy, faint not; but having renounced the hidden things of dishonesty, walking not in craftiness nor handling the word of God deceitfully, we preach the word, being instant in season and out of season, reproving, rebuking, exhorting with all longsuffering and doctrine. We declare the truth at all times; not compromising it to suit our hearers. Not saying one thing and thinking another. Our speech is yea and yea. We, who walk in the Spirit seek after sound doctrine and to be filled with the Spirit. Then we seek fellowship with those of like mind that we may be coworkers together with our Lord.

In these last days many will not endure sound doctrine, but after their own lusts shall they heap (gather) to themselves teachers having itching ears. The ears of hearers itch to hear something new. Like the Athenians, they like to hear and tell new things. They like to hear that which will entertain them and encourage them to remain at ease among God's people. They don't want to hear old truths that prick their conscience and demand response. The teachers know what itches their ears, and will give them what they want - devotional ministry that soothes their conscience and comforts them in their sin. Like their hearers they too have itching ears; ears that itch for praise. They rush to the exit of the hall at the close of a meeting, not to escape the maddening crowd but to enjoy the hearty hand shake and pat on the back with the words of praise - *'brother I enjoyed your word'*. To which a modest man will reply - *'take it as from the Lord'*. Oh, how he loves to muse on the truth - '*many are called but few chosen*', and pats his own back imagining that he is one of the few. But he loves not to pat the back of one truly chosen. He claims to walk in the light, but his conduct belies it, for he will not fellowship with those who bear witness to the truth in assemblies that are scripturally constituted and lawful. He will be observed moving in fellowships which are loose, liberal, large and where there is much flesh to which he can minister.

Normally, he enters upon his mission by mounting a platform to preach the gospel, claiming to be the Lord's messenger in the Lord's message. Soon self appears to express experiences and opinions, and it becomes apparent that he is his own messenger in his own message. He will con himself into thinking that the first person to make a profession as a result of his preaching is a token of the gift of evangelism, and in order to get more tokens he learns the art of persuading and influencing people to make professions, by preying on their emotions. Then he progresses to pressurizing people into premature professions by putting the fear of judgment into them. He glories in seeing one remain at the end of the meeting to make a profession.

Just as a fighter pilot marks the fuselage of his plane to let others know, he will mark it indelibly in his mind to let the brethren know. He will bring to their remembrance that A.N.Other was saved under his ministry in the bachwoods, way back 36 yrs ago on the 6th. of June at 6 o'clock. Just as six symbolises all of man, so also this man's ministry is all of man; for the glory of man. Nothing in it for God. It is of man; controlled and empowered by man, and regenerated with the praise of man.

Not content with preaching the gospel to sinners, he will seek the opportunity to teach the saints. In so doing he is claiming the double gift - one gift is not sufficient for him. He will mount the platform to preface his word of ministry by saying - *'all ministry should be for the Glory of God, Christ centred, and to the edification of the saints.'* Soon the simple saint will sense that very subtly self is slipping into the centre of the message, and the ministry is drifting into being devotional. This pleases both hearer and teacher, for most of it is directed away from the hearer and devoted to the teacher, but most of all it is directed away from the Lord Jesus Christ and definitely not for the Glory of God. His ministry is devoid of profit to the saint. It is dead, for it is not of the Spirit.

He that desires to carve out a name for himself does so in his own strength. As the wood on which one carves his name is dead, so also the works of one who carves out a name for himself in his own strength. Just as wood is consumed by fire, so also the dead works done in the flesh will be consumed by the judgment of the one whose eyes are as a flame of fire. Rev.1:14. His works will be burned up for they were done by the wrong means.

Such a self appointed teacher and preacher cannot love God; for only the Spirit filled Christian can love

God and his neighbour with love that is sacrificial - agape love. Instead he loves himself. He loves the preeminence; and he loves filling his diary with bookings for the years that lie ahead, and no love for the coming of the Lord. He loves the place of honour; he loves the double honour, and the sterling hand shake. He loves not to do without and wait by faith on our Lord providing. He has never been to Cherith where the brook dried up. He has arrived at Zarephath where the barrel of meal shall not be used up neither the cruise of oil. No hunger or thirst for him. He is beyond suffering want. He is beyond suffering reproach for His name. He has a form of godliness and of knowledge, and knows the truth in the law, and teaches others but not himself. Like the Pharasees he says and does not. c/f. Math.23:3.

Even though he is debtor to God and man, he is not inclined to love either. He is not inclined to be kind to any one, not even those in need. He is inclined to envy others especially those whom God has favoured. He is quick to boast of himself claiming to being favoured by God in winning many souls. Puffed up with pride in his abilities and capabilities he thinks more highly of himself than he ought. He ventures to express controversial opinions and in a manner that is not becoming a child of God. He seeks to make a name for himself among the brethren. He seeks not the welfare of others. Instead of seeing their need he can see the evil in them. He looks not within to see evil in himself. He does not bear the shortcomings of others and does not bear hearing of his own shortcomings. He has little hope of others being changed for good. He does not want to believe in others coming to believe in the Son of God. Nor does he want to endure the contradiction of others.

He lacks the control and power of the Holy Spirit who will constrain him to love God and his neighbour, and enable him to do right for the right motive. He needs to realize the truth of "Though I speak with the tongues of men and of angels, and have not love, I am become as sounding brass, or a tinkling cymbal. And though I have the gift of prophecy, and understand all mysteries, and all knowledge; and though I have all faith, so that I could remove mountains, and have not love, I am nothing. And though I bestow all my goods to feed the poor, and though I give my body to be burned, and have not love, it profiteth me nothing."1Cor.13:1-3

All work done for the wrong motive (love of self) is of no avail. It fails to create an anxious thought and sinners remain unmoved, unaffected, unchanged and unconverted. Not being rooted in love for God; it is as hay without root, dried up, fit only for the burning, for it fails to woo and win the unrighteous to righteousness.

He that loves himself more than the Lord has little or no love for his fellowman. He may love in word and tongue, but not in deed and truth. Talk is cheap but it takes love to move ones feet. To know to do good and not do it is sin and mars his fellowship with the Lord. His heart condemns him so that he is not open, transparent and upright in his dealings with others. He is crafty and given to using guile. He does not have a thirst for righteousness and since his heart is not wholly in the work he abounds not in doing good and soon tires. He does not minister to all but to those that show little resistance. Any good that he does it is not out of bounty but of covetousness. He covets the praise of man. Lacking love for his fellowman he is above giving of himself to do good. He is not above thinking more highly of himself than he ought and unwisely speaks of himself, seeking his own glory. He is not above saying anything that will offend, and prides himself in speaking his mind. Yet he does not take it kindly when others speak their mind and offend him. He is not above doing that which is unbecoming a child of God and may even raise his voice to win his point. He is arrogant and not given to forbearance so that he is not meek in his approach to sinners. Nor is he gracious and courteous but is impolite and disrespectful. Lacking boldness in the Spirit he does not stand up for the truth but compromises it. He speaks as pleasing men, even stoops to using flattery. Since he declares not the counsel of God he speaks not as one with authority but as one without assurance. He does not commend himself to the conscience of others. He does not find favour with the least favoured and finds it difficult to engage any in matters regarding faith in Christ. There is nothing dignified and winsome in his manner of conversation. It is neither fair or fruitful. There is no beauty in it that even the most beastly of men would desire. It is of no value to man and definitely of no value to God and just as stubble cannot be fed to the beasts of the field and cannot be used by man, it is fit for the burning, so also work done in a selfish manner is vain and unprofitable. It is fit for the burning.

At the Judgment seat of Christ the child of God will give account of himself to God.

All deeds done in the flesh will be as wood, consumed.

All deeds done in love for self will be as hay, consumed.

All deeds done in a selfish manner will be as stubble, consumed.

For we, children of God shall all stand before the judgment seat of Christ, as it is written – "I live saith the Lord, every knee shall bow to me, and every tongue shall confess to God; so then every one of us shall give account of himself to God." Rom.14:11-12. Each of us shall be judged according to our deeds, and "every man shall receive his own reward according to his own labour."1Cor.3:8. God shall bring every work into judgment with every secret thing, whether good or whether evil." Ecc.12:14.

We are sure that the judgment of God is according to truth, and God being just is no respecter of persons will judge impartially and in righteousness. With eyes as a flame of fire our Lord will see into and through each and every deed, and search out the means, the motive, and the manner of all work done. He will see into the deeds of the foolish servant, and see through the veneer of his righteousness, and judge that by self effort with love for himself and in a selfish manner he sought to carve out a name for himself. That child of God will bow to the judgment of the Lord, and confess it to be so. God will condemn and consume such work just as wood, hay, and stubble. There shall remain nothing to be rewarded.

All his time, talents, and treasure were sacrificed in vain. The foolish servant, not having paid the price for being filled with the Spirit, will pay the greater price, by not receiving any reward for his work done in the body (his own body and His body) cf 1Cor.5:10., and not receiving a crown of righteousness, and having nothing to lay at our Lord's feet. At the marriage of the Lamb he shall be arrayed in fine linen clean and white, yet not embroidered with righteousnesses as seen only by our Lord. "To obey is better than sacrifice" 1Sam.15:22. So be wise, and obey the Lord's command – "be filled with the Spirit." Eph.5:18.

The wise servant, having obeyed the Lord's command and having yielded himself and his members as instruments of righteousness unto God he will rejoice and be exceedingly glad for great shall be his reward. The Holy Spirit will continuously renew the humbleness of his mind and generate within him a hatred for the deeds of the self seekers, and regenerate his love for the Lord. He will not drift from his first love.

The Spirit of God will enable him to wisely overcome the inclination to being infatuated with self. He will decrease that the Lord might increase and possess His rightful place in that servant's heart; the place of preeminence. He will not tolerate evil doers and will try every spirit. He will not cease to teach and preach Jesus Christ in the public place and from house to house. Having the Spirit of power, love and a sound mind, he will overcome the inclination to being indecisive. He will purpose in his heart to wholly follow the Lord. He will serve the Lord with all his heart. He will resolve to stand up for the Lord and for the cause of righteousness, and for the truth at all times. He will not compromise the truth to suit his hearers, nor withhold the truth to avoid hostility. He will suffer affliction, persecution, tribulation, and imprisonment.

Even though he be thoroughly tried, he will not waver or weaken in his determination to serve the Lord. He will overcome the inclination to indulge in serving his own lusts. He will hold fast the Lord's name and the faithful word, that by sound doctrine both refute, and convince gainsayers. He will be bold in our God to speak the gospel of God with much contention, for his exhortation is not of deceit, nor of uncleanness, nor in guile. As one allowed of God to be put in trust with the gospel, he will speak not as pleasing men but God who trieth the heart. Neither at any time will he use flattering words, nor a cloak of covetousness. God is his witness.

Not of men will he seek glory; nor will he use his gift to profit self. He will overcome the inclination to busy himself in vain matters. He will busy himself in the work of the Lord, ever abounding in doing the good that he should and building up treasure in heaven, yea until the Lord returns. He will have a zeal for the things of God. He will not suffer those that would propagate false doctrine and seduce the people of God into embracing heresy and speaking lies in hypocrisy.

His stance for righteousness will not weaken and his interest and concern for others will not decline. He will overcome the inclination to being indifferent. He will devote less time to his own wants and devote his attention to the needs of others.

He will strengthen his interest in people, so much so that he will be ever ready to do good in season or out. He will overcome the inclination to insincerity, and will not put off until a more convenient time the good that he should do. He will not sit at home studying to show himself approved unto men in striving about the law and winning debates on how to do right.

Since the door of opportunity is ever open to do right, he will rise up and go through it and forth to climb the highest mountain and cross the cruelest sea in order to bring good tidings to a soul in need. He will overcome the inclination to inactivity that doth so easily beset us. Our Lord knows that His servant will not be wretched, miserable or poor, and He knows that His servant can see afar off and will be looking for the blessed hope and the glorious appearing of the great God and our Saviour Jesus Christ, and beyond to the Bema and the marriage of the Lamb.

"If then ye be risen with Christ, seek those things which are above, where Christ sitteth on the right hand of God. Set your affections on things above, not on things on the earth. For ye are dead, and your life is hid with Christ in God. When Christ, who is your life, shall appear, then shall ye also appear with Him in glory." Col.3"1-4. "Put on therefore, as the elect of God, holy and beloved, bowels of mercies, kindness and humbleness of mind, neekness, longsuffering; forbearing one another, and above all these things put on love, which is the bond of perfectness. and let the peace of God rule in your hearts, to which also ye are called in one body; and be thankful." Col.3:12-15. "And whatsoever ye do in word or deed, do all in the name of the Lord Jesus Christ, giving thanks to God and the Father by Him." Col.3:17. "And whatsoever ye do, do it heartily, as to the Lord, and not unto men; knowing that of the Lord ye shall receive the reward of your inheritance; for ye serve the Lord Jesus Christ." Col.3:23-24.

At the Bema all work done by the Divine means (in the Spirit) will abide longer than gold, for it will abide the life time of the eternal Spirit. All work done for the Divine motive (love for God) will abide longer than silver, for it will abide as long as love. All work done in the Divine manner that becometh the Son of God, will abide longer than precious stones for it will radiate the life time of the Son of God.

Whilst we are still in the flesh, and realizing that we were not redeemed with corruptible things such as silver and gold from our vain manner of conversation, but with the precious blood of our Lord, we pass the time of our sojourn in fear of displeasing our Lord, "and seeing we are compassed about with so great a cloud of witnesses, let us lay aside every weight and the sin that doth so easily beset us and let us run with patience the race that is set before us." He.12:1 Yea, for the joy that is set before us of seeing our Lord the author and finisher of our faith, endure our cross despising the shame, and lest we be wearied and faint in our minds consider Him who endured such contradiction of sinners against Himself." Heb.12:1-3

Let us speak forth for God not with a haughty spirit, but be poor in spirit, then we can comfort them who mourn and we shall be kept meek to possess all the earth without it possessing us. Let us hunger and thirst to do right at all times and our lives will be filled with opportunities and God who has been merciful to us will further be merciful and enable us to show mercy to others. With pure hearts, free of imperfections and perfect with God we shall see and know the Lord God. Let us like Caleb with another Spirit, wholly follow the Lord and possess our possessions, and wholeheartedly exclaim – "Give Me That Mountain" that place high above all in thought, word and deed; above all in love, life and happiness.

Then, having overcome and conquered all that would oppose us from entering that rest of God, each of us like the apostle Paul recall saying –I have fought a good fight; I have finished my course; I have kept the faith, hence forth is laid up for me a crown of righteousness" 2Tim.4:7-8, and in love for the Lord's coming, be ready to be offered up, the Spirit of God testifying with our spirit that before our departure we had this testimony, that we pleased God.

Then we will have an abundantly sweet entrance into the presence of the Lord God.

It will be sweet to know that we are safe at last: safe and sound in the presence of the Lord.

It will be sweet to see Him as He is and be like Him

It will be sweet to hear Him say - 'well done my good and faithful servant'

It will be sweet to be crowned for having loved the Lord and been faithful in trials, in enduring temptation, in suffering and in striving for mastery of doing right the right way.

It will be sweet to enter into paradise and to eat of the tree of eternal life, and relish the hidden manna (sweet communion with the Lord). Then to receive the power (right) to rule. Then to rejoice in the white raiment suitably entwined with his righteousnesses, and then to rejoice in the position as a pillar in the temple of God and in his place with our Lord on His throne.

What a privilege it will be to lay our crowns at His feet, for they are His by right.

Such position, power, possessions, and privileges and such a prize no man ever deserved, yet this is our right by birth into the family of God.

Will we receive our birthright in vain?

Will we receive our birthright to gain and win the battle for right, and win the unrighteous to righteousness and win the prize for fulfilling our purpose of being created and win the prize of the high calling of God in Christ ?                    We were

## BORN AGAIN TO WIN

Printed in the United States
By Bookmasters